DESTINY

Paintings by the author

Katharine Patience Hague – Selected Watercolours

www.slideshare.net

Slide presentation of B&W photographs

Katharine Patience Hague
Biographical Photographs 1916-1960

www.slideshare.net

Website dedicated to the author

www.lhague.plus.com

DESTINY

My Life from WW1 to WW2

KATHARINE PATIENCE HAGUE

Edited by Lynette Hague

KIDBROOKE PRESS

Published in the UK by Kidbrooke Press

www.kidbrookepress.com

ISBN 978-1-8383220-0-7

CHAPTERS

PHOTOGRAPHS
Over 100 B&W photos are interspersed between chapters

EPILOGUE

REMINISCENCES

ADDENDA
Parents, People, Books and Places

FOREWORD

In early 2007, at the age of 91, my mother wrote the story of the first half of her life because she thought it interesting. She wrote it in an old A4 notebook with hardly any correction. I typed it up as she went along. Although she died on 12th December 2008 it is only now that I have been able to put it into book form.

We have quite a number of old black and white photographs which are used to illustrate the story. This is not something my mother had envisaged.

Lynette Hague
May 2021

1

38 WESTCOMBE PARK ROAD, BLACKHEATH

1915

On the day that I was born, 8th June 1915, the Western world was ablaze. The Great War had been raging for nearly a year. The second battle at Ypres was at its height. In May the first gas attacks by the Germans on the Western Front had created ripples of horror around the 'civilized' world. On 7th May the sinking of the Lusitania had become front page news and the number of allied casualties rose to over 400,000. The whole nature of warfare was changing. Trench warfare was beginning on the battle grounds of Ypres. U-boats were soon to be informing the USA that henceforth neutral ships would be acceptable targets as the noose tightened round Britain, causing severe shortages and rationing. By 1915 Zeppelins had started dropping bombs on London causing many civilian casualties.

In the midst of this conflagration a drama on a smaller scale was being enacted in the house at 38 Westcombe Park Road, London. Life was in the balance for one small baby. The apparently lifeless body was wrapped in cotton wool and placed on the window sill while doctor and midwife were faced with the urgent needs of the mother. It was some time later that thoughts returned to the newborn infant, which was then discovered to be alive.

It is difficult for us to look back to those times and imagine the kind of patriotism that enthused the nation, that sent young men in their thousands rushing to enlist to fight for king and country. The Edwardian world of the middle classes, cocooned in all that the British Empire had brought it, still lived in a euphoria of idealism remote from reality. A breath of fresh air could be felt when Edward VII came to the throne. The industrial revolution and expansion of the Empire had brought ideas of luxury and freedom to Britain which were then to be crushed by the dreadful reality of war.

The reluctance to incarnate of the new arrival at No.38 then manifested in loud protestations. 'Nurse' in those times reigned supreme and laid down strict rules of behaviour – the infant must never be lifted other than for changing and feeding. Missing the warmth and security of the mother's womb the baby voiced her feelings of abandonment in no uncertain terms. Finally, when she broke a blood vessel in her throat, the doctor issued stern instructions that on no account must she be left to cry.

The early optimism that the war would soon be over gradually changed. By 1916 the bombardments of London from the air were becoming ever more frequent. It was a long time before some form of defence against these attacks was devised and in the meantime much damage was caused.

The raids became so bad that it was arranged for our nurse to take my sister and me to stay in a safe seaside town. With a little foresight it could have been seen as a situation filled with danger. A young person was given responsibility for two small children, one five years old and the other not yet two, with no respite, no days off. Unfortunate but obvious, therefore, that her temper would get frayed and self-preservation would impose certain disciplines and practices. Physical chastisement would become too severe. It was easier to take the older child to the seaside in the afternoon and leave the younger one to cry herself to sleep. Many children receive far worse treatment than this, yet for one small child this experience left a legacy of nightmares, bedwetting and insecurity that lasted for years.

2

FAIRLAWN, KIDBROOKE GROVE, BLACKHEATH

1919 - 1923

My earliest clear memory is of our first visit to the house that was to become our home. It was an empty shell, yet inviting and friendly. Quite on my own – as usual – I climbed some steps to a side door overlooking a courtyard and began a tour of inspection. Opening doors and peering into empty rooms at last I came upon the door that opened into the bathroom. Here was a room all ready for use. Racing down the stairs I proclaimed to the empty air, "I've found the bathroom!"

We spent four years in that happy house and garden. When furnished it glowed with pride. The L-shaped hall had a polished floor leading to wide wooden stairs. A complete suite of armour stood by the lobby that led to the front door. In the light and airy drawing room was a big round table on which were interesting knick-knacks and photos in silver frames. Best of all was the dark and mysterious study with deep red walls lined with shelves of books. It had an inviting open fireplace. Then there was the dining room with its dark, carved wooden table and chairs. French windows opened out onto a simple lawn surrounded by shrubs. Here the puppies were brought out to play as soon as they could walk. Dogs have always been a part of our family and my mother even took her current pooch on her honeymoon with her.

It may seem strange to spend so much time talking of the house and garden, but at that time this was the real world. These are abiding memories for me.

Injustice

My sister, Peggy, was three years older than me. She arrived in a world still at peace. There was time for a proper bonding between the parents and their first-born child. She was 'Bubsie,' and there are many photos to show her steady progress. For me there was the feeling of being a spectator watching from the sidelines. This was enhanced by the way it was impressed upon me that being the youngest child meant being excluded from certain activities and happenings. That in turn caused me to be at times rebellious at what seemed unfairness and injustice in the treatment meted out to me.

Speaking delayed

Because of my unhappy experiences at the hands of our nurse during the war my development suffered a setback. My speaking was delayed and, to make matters worse, I became friendly with a Down's boy, mimicking his ways to the extent that my poor parents began to believe that their offspring had learning difficulties.

Standing on the fringe

Behind the house was the vegetable garden. Spaced out between fruit trees and gooseberry bushes were rows of potatoes, carrots and peas. Beyond was a high hedge with a gate that led to an uncultivated area. This was our playground, complete with swing and sand pit. My sister used to bring her friends to play while I would stand on the fringe and watch. Once they started to dig a large hole in an attempt to reach Australia by way of a short cut. This idea filed me with dread horror. Nothing would prevail upon me to go near or peer into the depths.

Activities with my father

I was four years old when we moved into Fairlawn. The war was over and everywhere people were trying to come to terms with peace, which was so far removed from their pre-war lives. For us, we suddenly became aware of a father figure. My father, a quiet, self-contained man, filled me with awe. He was determined to take his responsibilities seriously and thought up many ways of entertaining us. Often he would take Peggy and me across Blackheath Common to Greenwich Park. Here we walked between rows of tall trees right up to the clock at the top, which displayed for all the world to see Greenwich Mean Time. There my father would solemnly set his watch.

We sailed our boats on the pond and flew our kites. Back at home we would jump on our pogo sticks or skip with our skipping ropes. It was at these times that I really felt a part of the family. At other times the feeling of tagging along became oppressive.

One occasion stands out when my father bought me a bicycle for my seventh birthday. He taught me to ride by taking me to the top of the road outside our house, placing me firmly in the saddle, telling me to hold on tight, and then giving me a hard push down the hill. I sailed dizzily down to the bottom, crossed the road at the end and came to a halt half way up the hill opposite. I could ride!

My father was a real Londoner. On our many visits up to town we never took a taxi or rode on a bus. My father knew every back street and alley. He had a long stride for such a short man and we had difficulty keeping up with him – but it all seemed an adventure to us! We quite often ended up in Tottenham Court Road at the entrance to Shearns, a vegetarian food shop with a large restaurant reached by climbing some rickety stairs up to the first floor. Sometimes we visited the Science Museum and then, of course, there were the Christmas Lectures at the Royal Institution. Here we sat in the darkness on long wooden benches and thrilled at all the colourful experiments being played out before us.

Social life

My parents led a fairly full social life. Friends would be invited for a meal in the evenings and I would lie in bed and listen to their voices and the infectious sound of my mother's laughter. I can still picture my mother in a beautiful blue dress on her way out to a party. Still ringing out in my memory, even now, are songs from the latest shows which could be heard around the house after their visits to the theatre. *The Quaker Girl* was a favourite.

Our own lives, ruled over by a governess, were remote from most of all this. But with summer came welcome weekends when we would drive out into the countryside for picnics amongst the gorse and bracken. There were plenty of lovely beauty spots to choose from in the early twenties. Thick woods and common land spread over much of Kent and Sussex. Names come to mind such as Foots Cray, St Paul's Cray, St Mary's Cray, Sidcup, Seven Oaks, Hildenborough, Westerham and Wrotham. They call up memories of halcyon summer days when butterflies and birds, rabbits and even the occasional deer were our companions. Keston Ponds was memorable as home to a family of swans, fiercely territorial. Many a dog had ended its life in an uneven battle with these birds.

My father came from a large family, having six brothers and three sisters, and we gradually got to know our aunts and uncles and numerous cousins on those idyllic excursions. I have a photo of three Bullnose Morris cars lined up together, ready to convey us all to our selected venue. Once there rugs would be spread over a suitable spot and the hamper opened to display sandwiches, hard boiled eggs, fruit and cake.

My favourite cousin was Jan, my godmother's son. In my eyes he was quite grown up. He eventually became a pilot, serving on one of the first aircraft carriers. He was killed when his release mechanism failed and he plunged with his aircraft into the sea.

My mother, by contrast, was the only child of an Irish artist who died when I was only four. She never knew her own mother who died shortly after giving birth. However she did have an aunt Nora in Australia who came to visit occasionally.

Father a photographer

My father was a keen photographer and always took his camera with him on these excursions. It was his pride to process his own films. We always had a dark room with shelves of mysterious bottles filled with developer, fixative and other strange chemicals. On the bench were small porcelain dishes just the right size to take the exposed glass plates holding the magic pictures that came from the camera. Then there were the little wooden frames into which the 'developed' plate would be fitted with the printing paper and placed against the window for the light to create the final printed picture.

Activities with my mother

My mother loved her flower garden and was a first class dressmaker. She made all our clothes for us when we were young. As we children grew older we were able to join her in her inexhaustible enthusiasm for making things to sell at fairs and bazaars to raise money for different charities to do with animal welfare. Amongst other things we learnt to make artificial flowers, pin cushions, needle cases and all kinds of doll's clothes.

Vegetarianism

Because of illness my parents had become vegetarians. This developed into a concern for animal welfare and we were surrounded by anti-vivisection literature and information about various animal charities. My sister and I became known as cranks until we went to a vegetarian boarding school.

Magnetic healer

My sister suffered from inflamed tonsils and adenoids and was taken the round of specialists in the hope of finding a cure for her. I can remember sitting on the sidelines while she was being treated. On one occasion I watched with great interest while a magnetic healer, Dr Lovell, massaged, tapped and stroked her face, nose and neck with great success. Her nose ran like a tap! Of course I had to partake of any diet that was prescribed. Whereas she hated them all, I found them really palatable.

First school

Memories from my early school days are extremely vague and I can remember only two incidents from my first school. One happened on my very first day. We were mounting the steep stairs in pairs when my partner said something to me. I had just started to reply to her – with no notion that we were breaking a rule – when the teacher suddenly called me to her and took me to the head mistress's room. She made me sit on a humpty pouffe, scolding me all the while. I stayed in that empty, terrifying place for what seemed an eternity.

The second episode happened at the end of the day when a group of small children were waiting at the school gates to be taken home. One boy, whose face is the only one of all the teachers and pupils I can remember, began to bully the girls. They were crying and getting really upset. Then, quite suddenly, he turned on me and tried to pull my hair. What happened next was as much a surprise and shock to me as to any one there. I exploded in a rage and attacked him, hitting him hard over the head with such force that he ran away in terror.

Filled with satisfaction and confidence at the outcome of this encounter, I began to wonder what had happened to 'Ginger' Greaves, my governess, who should have arrived to pick me up from school. Still buoyed up by my recent victory I started off on the homeward journey by myself. I didn't get very far before there came the vision of Ginger careering towards me on her bike. She was beside herself with anger, having arrived at school to find me gone and teachers ignorant of my whereabouts. I was hauled back to school to apologise for causing such distress – but I have never been able to quieten a voice that told me that if she had not been late there would not have been such an upset.

Second school

My second school was no more memorable than the first. St Helen's was an attractive house set in a pleasant garden, but I have no recollection of a classroom, teacher or pupil. My only memory is of the dining room. I must have been staying the whole day at school and therefore eating my lunch there. Being vegetarian I could only eat the vegetables, but what stays in my memory is the strange smell of cooked meat and fish. That is all that remains in my mind. I made no friends and no teacher influenced me.

Piano lessons

One teacher I *can* remember from my time in Blackheath was our piano teacher. Each week Peggy and I would be taken to Miss Davis' house at the top of the village. While Peggy had her lesson I would sit at the table with a large glass of milk and a biscuit. After half an hour we would change places and I would have my lesson.

Dancing and elocution lessons

We also attended ballroom dancing classes in the Town Hall run by a very imposing lady called Mrs Grant. Peggy must also have had elocution lessons or something like that for I can remember one exciting occasion when she was to perform on the stage. For several weeks she had been learning a poem to recite. By the time of the performance I knew it as well as she did. Even now parts of it will come unbidden into my mind: 'Up the airy mountain, down the rushy glen…'

The day came. We were in the front row near the steps up to the stage. The theatre was packed full of children and their parents. Then Peggy's name was called out and she stood up to take her coat off – but before she could move I had leapt up the stairs and stood at the corner of the stage. There was a sudden hush and my voice was heard loud and clear:

> A beetle got stuck in the jam,
> He cried, "Oh how unhappy I am!"
> His Ma said, "Don't talk, if you really can't walk
> You'd better go home in a tram."

Who taught me this jingle I really can't say, but it got a very good response from the audience. I was six years old.

On my own

I must have been a disappointment to my parents. They, of course, had hoped for a boy. Instead they found themselves with an awkward, shy child who on the one hand seemed to live in a dream world of her own and yet at times could be unreasonable and demanding.

Unable to make friends of my own, I spent most of my time by myself. Sometimes I would wander down Kidbrooke Grove and meet the milk cart coming up the hill. It stopped by each house to deliver the milk straight out of huge churns. There were no bottles or cartons in those days. The maid came with a jug or can and the milkman would choose the right size ladle to pour the measured amount into the jug. I would be allowed to squeeze onto the platform and ride up in style. The horse was so used to the routine that just a cluck from the milkman and he would be on his way again.

Sometimes I would take my doll out for an airing in my beautiful new pram – not that I was too keen on playing with dolls. It was the smooth way the wheels covered the ground, its highly polished sides and gleaming metal that filled me with joy.

Object of undivided attention

Looking back on those years of early childhood I can say with truth that the most memorable experience happened quite by chance. My parents were preparing to take us to Totnes in Devon for a summer holiday when I inconveniently fell ill with a fever. It might have been measles, but it was bad enough for the study to be turned into a sickroom and a fire lighted in the open grate. I can remember lying in the dark while the flames made moving patterns on the ceiling. Because I was in no condition to travel on the appointed day it was decided that Peggy should not miss any of her holiday and she and our nurse should go on ahead. There could have been a no more contended child in the world than me as I revelled in the unaccustomed experience of having all the attention centred on me. When it was considered safe for me to travel I was wrapped up warmly in the back of the car and we set out on the long journey to Devon.

FAIRLAWN, KIDBROOKE GROVE, BLACKHEATH

We had been travelling for some considerable time when my mother looked behind her to see me with tears pouring down my face. I was so cold that I was shivering. It was quickly decided that we must stay at the next hotel we came to. It was getting dark as we drove into Alresford and stopped before the Swan Inn. Bright lights greeted us, then wide stairs led up to mysterious dark passages. Luxurious thick carpet softened our footsteps. Soon a warm bed enfolded me and sleep came before it was possible to digest the full extent and magnificence of my first unforgettable adventure in the great outside world – the object of both my parents' undivided attention!

Fell into the weir

We loved going to Totnes. We got up early in the morning to skip down the hill to the dairy for the Devonshire cream, the intoxicating smell of newly baked bread invading our nostrils. We had trips in a rowing boat on the river Dart, when I always insisted on taking my turn with oars.

Once we were walking along the wall of the weir with the dark, speeding water on one side. As usual I was trailing some way behind the rest of the family when suddenly I lost my footing and found myself in the water, holding on to the wall of the weir. The pressure of the water was forcing me against the stone but also trying to drag me along and under. How long I stayed gripping a ledge that providentially presented itself I don't know. Here was a dark green world surrounding me and shutting me away from the familiar world of light, air and family. It was strange to hear my father's voice quite clearly say, "Where's Pat?" It can't have taken him long to retrace his steps, find me, and pull me out of the murky depths.

Lost at the fair

My habit of trailing along behind the family introduced me to another adventure when I was still quite small. We had gone to the heath where a fair was in progress. The whole area was covered with booths, coconut shies, swings and roundabouts. It was packed with excited crowds come to enjoy all the fun of the fair. Quite suddenly I found myself alone, my family had completely disappeared! This seemed to be a fairly usual occurrence and well catered for. Quite quickly my troubles were identified and a friendly person took care of me. I was led to the huge iron gates of Greenwich Park and just inside, at the back of the gates, was a section cordoned off with a chain. There I had a miserable wait until my parents came to claim me.

Dogs – Coo-ee and Chris

Dogs were an important part of my mother's life. While at Fairlawn she acquired a wire-haired bitch called Coo-ee. She was a pedigree dog with a really long name, but to us she was Coo-ee. My mother was hoping to breed from Coo-ee and show her best dogs at Crufts. We loved the puppies when they arrived and would spend hours playing with them.

One Christmas eve a guest came to our door. It was a long-haired English sheepdog – dirty, bedraggled and emaciated. We fed him and cleaned him up, untangled the knots in his long coat and petted him. From a cowed and frightened scarecrow he became a sleek and elegant hound of great character and a good sense of humour.

Of course we had to report him to the authorities so that his owner could claim him. But days turned to weeks and we began to think of him as part of the family. But then the fateful day came when his owner was at the door. An uncouth, rough-looking farmer claimed him as his own and Chris was unwillingly dragged away. We wept but could only watch him go.

Unbelievably he came back with a broken chain about his neck. Once more a scraggy mess with open sores and every evidence of brutal treatment. Of course the farmer knew where to come to retrieve him. My mother begged to be able to buy him. She was willing to pay anything to save him. But this cold-hearted ruffian refused to listen to her pleas. We never saw Chris again.

Fledgling cuckoo

There was another guest that came to stay with us for a while. I was in the garden one day when I came upon a baby bird that had fallen from its nest. As it seemed very much alive and demanding sustenance we brought it in and fed it bread soaked in milk on the end of a matchstick. As it continued to thrive on our treatment my mother bought a bird cage for it and it was hung outside the kitchen door. As it grew we were amazed to find that we had become the owners of a fledgling cuckoo.

A problem arose when we were due to go on our summer holidays. What could we do with our cuckoo? Our next door neighbours lived in a big house which had a large garden looked after by a gardener. On being asked if he would care for our bird he agreed, but had no idea of how to look after it. He put it in the greenhouse where it lived all by itself. The poor little thing pined away and by the time we came back it was dead.

Locked in

Another experience which occurred around about that time demonstrates my feelings of insecurity and dread of being confined which was left over from the time our nurse locked me in the bedroom while taking Peggy down to the sea. Peggy had a great friend called Mona. She was a lively little girl with bright sparkling black eyes and dark curly hair held back neatly with a velvet ribbon. I liked her a lot so when Peggy was persuaded to take me with her to play at Mona's house I was very willing to go.

On our arrival Peggy and Mona disappeared and I was taken upstairs to the nursery and introduced to a small boy two or three years younger than me. Worse – far worse – happened very quickly. I turned to see the door being closed by the retreating nurse and then, horror of horrors, I could hear the key turning in the lock! I leapt to the door and banged on it with all my might while screaming to be let out. As soon as the door was opened I rushed down the stairs and out of the house. I didn't stop running until the safety of our home was reached.

My friend Violet

Having reached the age of seven I became more aware of life around me and even found a friend of my own. On the opposite side of our road there stood a large house, rather dark and gloomy, hidden amongst tall trees. It was a maternity home run by two doctors, Dr White and Dr Pink. It was very well known and women came from far and wide to have their babies delivered there.

Dr White had two daughters, Helen and Violet. As Peggy and Helen became friends, being of the same age, so I became friends with Violet. We began to have adventures together. Their garden was a mysterious place full of dark corners filled with ferns and untidy shrubs. There were the remains of an old greenhouse or conservatory covered with moss and lichen where an old toad lived. We spent endless happy hours investigating this strange world together.

Conversation with old man

About this time I had another happy meeting. Alongside our garden was an alleyway lined on either side with a high wooden lap fence. It led all the way from Blackheath village to Shooters Hill. In the early morning and evening it was filled with men trudging to and from work. At other times it was a quiet little lane that I often explored by myself.

One day, as I was meandering along, it being a cool refuge from the hot summer sun, a broken part of the fence attracted my attention. The grounds of Morden Cottage, an almshouse for old men, spread out before me. Standing quite near and regarding me with interest was a little old man with a mop of white hair learning on a stick. He beckoned me towards him so I climbed through the hole in the fence. He led me to a wooden bench where we sat and talked. This was the one and only meeting we had together. There is no recollection of the content of our conversation. Our meeting remained a precious secret, the memory of a friendship never to be forgotten.

Mother, Pat and sister Peggy at roadside

Near Chalfont St Peter - Pat and her sister Peggy

Cotman's Ash, 20 May 1923 - Mother, Pat and Peggy

St Paul's Cray Common, May 1925

Totnes Castle, 4 August 1922

Berry Pomeroy Castle, 13 August 1922

Peggy, father and Pat

Dressed for a play - Pat as Prince Charming and Audrey Rice as Cinderella

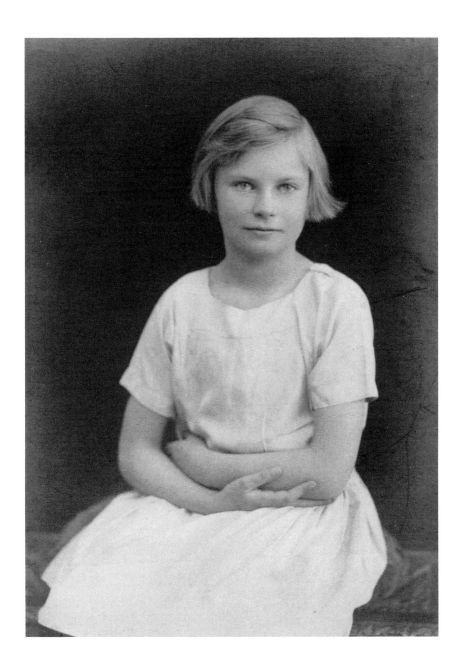

Three Bullnose Morris cars at Beaulieu Abbey, Hampshire - father on right

Violet with Peggy Pony and dog

3

Beechbrook, Lubbock Road, Chislehurst

1923 - 1928

I was eight years old when we moved to Chislehurst in order to be further away from London. The house stood at the bottom of a steep hill in a road with houses on either side. Behind the house the garden dropped sharply down to Lower Camden Road at the bottom. There was a brook with high banks which sectioned off the vegetable patch, garage and stables from the rest of the garden.

Beechbrook was three stories high with a cellar. The first night in our new house became a nightmare. We were awakened by sounds that were unmistakably those of shunting railway trucks. We discovered – to our horror – that behind the rows of houses lining Lower Camden Road was a steep embankment at the top of which ran the mainline railway between London and the coast. But, funnily enough, after the first few days of agony the time came by the end of the week when we slept through all the noise and were never troubled with it for the rest of the four years we lived there.

Beechbrook was not nearly so friendly as our little house in Blackheath and had long cold rooms. We had to climb some steps to reach the side door and a path from the road came sharply down through a shrubbery to the back door. This ushered you into a dark, flag-stoned scullery. Three floors up you came to the bedroom of Mr and Mrs Mac, our beloved cook and gardener. There was also a long corridor ending in a little room that eventually became my bedroom. This was the area that was my very own, where I spread out my railway lines and farmyard. My clockwork engines pulled the trucks the length of the corridor, bringing them to the neatly laid out station encircled by the farm with all its horses, cattle and sheep.

Quite a large garden surrounded the house, probably not as big as at Fairlawn, but it was about three quarters of an acre. The most interesting part for me was the stream that ran right from one side to the other, disappearing into a tunnel under the road. It had high banks on either side and many happy hours were spent exploring its length. To cross the stream it was necessary to use one of three small bridges. One, at the far end of the garden, was simply two planks spanning the banks. The one directly below the house, at the other end of the garden, was a complicated contraption made of flimsy laths with hand rails. The one that led to the garage and stables was more sturdy and served as the main access to the vegetable garden.

Rescued Coo-ee

We were to discover that the stream had unforeseen dangers. When the weather was bad and there had been a lot of rain the water would rise to the top of the banks. Then the owner of sluice gates far up at some undiscovered point would suddenly open his gates and release a torrent of water the length of all the intermediary back gardens and flood our entire vegetable plot. This happened one dark and stormy night when one of our dogs was found to be missing. I went round the back of the house in search of her and began to hear faint cries. Following their direction I found poor Coo-ee clinging to the bank with her head just above the water raging past her. I think I pulled her out just in time!

Coed Bel School (third school)

Peggy and I went to a small girls' school at the top of our road. My memory of Coed Bel School is very hazy. I can just remember my classroom and the fact that we played lacrosse rather than netball or hockey. Peggy gained a reputation for bravery by retaliating in kind when the small and fiery Madamoiselle slapped her across the face in the French lesson.

I have a photograph of Audrey Rice and me dressed in costume for Cinderella where I played the part of Prince Charming, but I have no memory of the performance. Although I came in for some teasing I also made some friends and used to play with Mary Munroe. Once she even came to stay, but when bedtime arrived she was so homesick and set up such a wail that her parents had to fetch her home.

Another time two or three of us were playing in the garden and decided to perform a play for the benefit of our parents. We bought sticky buns and lemonade for refreshments, invited the other parents, and then told my mother of our intentions. She very nearly had a heart attack, but rallied round sufficiently to be able to receive her guests in the drawing room with more suitable tea, sandwiches and cake.

Friendly with neighbours' boys

Apart from friends made at school I also played with children living nearby. Next door lived Dick Baines. He was away at boarding school for most of the year but when he was home we spent endless hours swopping cigarette cards.

There were two young boys who lived on the other side of Lower Camden Road. They were twins, but totally different in looks, temperament and behaviour. Buster, a small replica of his father, was fair, squat and pugnacious. Tim was dark, quiet and nervous just like his mother.

To get from our garden to theirs we paddled through the tunnel under the road. Coming up from the darkness into their garden was like entering another world. There was an air of neglect and decrepitude about the place. Mrs Scott looked drab and untidy. She always seemed tired and worn out. Mr Scott was continually shouting and swearing. The contrast between this and my own secure and well-ordered existence was extreme and was a shock to my sensibilities.

Dancing continued

There were other experiences of the larger world outside that came with varying impacts.

We continued to attend the dancing classes with Mrs Grant. It wasn't necessary to go to Blackheath because she also gave lessons in the Bell Hotel in Bromley. I have a recollection of being clasped to the satin-clad bosom of a helper as we waltzed around the room.

Swimming

We went to private swimming baths where we were taught to swim. The only other pupils besides Peggy and me were two sisters about my age. They were twins but very different in character. Patsy was a quiet, well-behaved girl but Bunty was quite different – a type of girl I had never met before! She was fair haired and tubby, and to me she seemed very spoilt. She wanted her own way all the time and her voice was continually raised in tantrums and protestations. I found it hard to believe anyone could behave so badly!

Riding

After we had been living in Chislehurst for about a year it was decided that we each should take up a hobby. Two possibilities were presented. Peggy chose golf and I decided that I would like to ride. There were riding stables just at the other end of Lower Camden Road and they soon became the centre of my life. I was free to spend my time there getting to know all the horses. Every Saturday morning Mr English, my teacher, would come to pick me up from our house.

There were usually three or four of us. To begin with I rode a pony on a leading rein, but as soon as my teacher was sure that I could control my mount we were left free to follow as we felt inclined. I say 'we' because now I am talking about Jumbo and me. Jumbo was an enormous ex-army horse. He was so experienced that he was really in charge. He liked to lag behind the group and go his own independent way. He had a game he used to play. If he found a pebble in the road he would kick it with his hoof and zig-zag following it.

To be alone with Jumbo gave me a wonderful feeling of independence and freedom. Later on it was time to say goodbye to Jumbo and I was given a beautiful pony called Princess. She was swift and temperamental but also sweet-natured and a wonderful ride. The urban nature of our surroundings with the tarmac-covered roads did not help to make our going very exciting, but there was a sandy rise leading up to Chislehurst Common where we could stretch our horses legs in a gallop that made us feel more adventurous.

Dogs again

At home our lives were much involved with animals of a different kind. Coo-ee, our rough-haired fox terrier, soon produced another litter of puppies and before long five bundles of trouble were roaming free in the garden. Johnny, the greediest pup, was so fond of his food that he was capable of guzzling until his tummy touched the ground. He was very partial to strawberries and one day he crawled under the netting to reach this favoured snack. Unfortunately, by the time he wanted to retreat his expanded size had become firmly stuck. As his shrieks and yelps could be heard from a great distance rescue was not a problem! Of this litter my mother retained two pups, Sally and George, so we now had three excitable dogs to feed, groom, exercise, and engage in play.

Right at the top of Lubbock Road, in one of the largest houses, there lived a man who owned a smart carriage, a kind of curricle drawn by two high spirited horses. Every morning a coachman drove him to the station in this curricle, a large hound running along beneath. This was the high point of our dogs' day. As this vision from the past came down the full length of Lubbock Road, turning sharply at the bottom of the hill and continuing along Lower Camden Road, our dogs would follow their progress on the inside of the garden fence, filling the air with their ear-splitting protestations and indignation. The baying and barking was indescribable and continued until the equipage had completely disappeared. Unfortunately there came a day when George, our macho defender, somehow escaped into the road and charged into battle. We think that the butt end of the coachman's whip made contact with the skull of our small hero for he soon began to suffer from fits and got so bad that finally he had to be put to sleep.

Relatives visited

It was around my ninth birthday that I began to be aware of the wider world beyond my immediate family. My grandmother would visit us at least once a month, coming down by train from the London hotel where she lived. She was a small, dominant figure dressed in black down to her ankles. Her hair was beautifully coiffed by M. Maurice using the kind of special hairpiece he fashioned for Queen Mary. She always brought a beautiful iced walnut cake from Fuller's and added to our appreciation of her visits by giving us each half a crown pocket money.

There was some mystery about her parentage. Rumour had it that she was the daughter of an alcoholic farmer and used to earn her living as a housekeeper. It was not clear if she actually worked for the Goolden family, but she married my grandfather and brought nine children into the world. He was a maths teacher at the prestigious Tonbridge School in Kent. Then, being something of a genius at invention, he went into business with a partner. However he wasn't as clever in business as at invention and was beset with money worries and stress prior an early death from an accident. He was running for a tram when he missed his footing and was injured. Unfortunately the injury became gangrenous and shortly afterwards he died. The two eldest sons, Walter and my father, Archie, were left to pick up the pieces. They supplied the finances for the education of the younger members of the family. Later they saw to the needs of their mother in her old age.

Uncle Walter and aunt Lucy lived on the other side of Chislehurst Common. My uncle and father were in constant communication by telephone owing to their mutual interest in the Sunday Times Torquemada crossword puzzles and an ongoing chess game. They played this by means of pocketbook chess sets.

When Walter was young, so the story goes, he fell in love with Lucy Plater, the daughter of a rich businessman. Walter was planning to be an engineer but that did not suit his future farther-in-law. "If you want to marry my daughter you'll have to join me in the stock exchange," he was told. Much against his inclinations, that is what he did.

He was the only man I knew who wore a bow tie, and he had a party trick of suddenly displaying his false teeth! His garden was his pride and joy, having a wonderful and colourful display of gladioli and dahlias in the summer months. Walter and Lucy had no children but, perhaps to make up for this lack, they owned an enormous black retriever that seemed quite out of place in their neat, well-ordered little house. His tail was just at the right height to sweep across the tea table with the distinct risk of disaster.

Lucy's sister, Evie, was the more well-upholstered of the two. She lived with her husband, Gerald, and son, Tim, within easy reach of her sister. Tim was quite a bit older than Peggy and me, but we were fond of him and he spent quite a bit of time in our house. He had a weepy eye and died an early death from tuberculosis.

Another young man who came to stay at regular intervals was our cousin Jan Nicholson, the son of aunt Kitty, my godmother. Harry and Kitty lived in India so maybe Jan looked on us as a second home. For the same reason Marjory and Douglas often spent their holidays with us as their parents, Cyril and Tinny, lived in Ceylon. Both children went to school in England, Douglas to a Blue Coat school and Marjory to a convent school in East Grinstead.

There were plenty of high jinks when all the young folk were around, practical jokes and teasing. I remember one occasion when Marjorie came down from her bedroom in distress and confessed that she had a rash that could be measles. She was very sorry that she hadn't told aunt Netta that she was actually in quarantine. Poor girl, she needn't have confessed, for the boys had put itching powder in her pyjamas!

Books

Because I was the youngest of them all I was not really part of the group and at this stage of my life I retired more and more into the world of books. My strongest memory of my father was his introduction to us of the joys to be had from reading. Most evenings when we were alone he would find the time to read to us. We had Stanley Weyman, Rudyard Kipling, *Old St Paul's*, *At the Back of the Northwind*, *The Arabian Nights*, to mention just a few of the well known books. There was also *Hajji Baba* by James Morier. We not only read *Alice in Wonderland* and *Alice Through the Looking Glass* but also *Sylvie and Bruno* by Lewis Caroll; not only *Tarzan the Ape Man* by Edgar Rice Burroughs, but also *A Princess of Mars* and other stories by the same author.

From this beginning came my own exploration into the literature on offer. I buried myself in fairy stories, myths and legends. The story of Finn, the Irish hero, was a great favourite, as was King Arthur and his knights of the Round Table. Then of course there was *Robin Hood*.

First camera

My father was always a distant figure and I have no recollection of him before my fourth birthday. When he was home he was either in his workroom fiddling with his wireless or in the garage working on his car. My actual encounters with him were few and far between. The episode of teaching me to ride a bicycle on my seventh birthday is one landmark. Another unforgettable occasion must have been on another birthday. He had taken me to London to buy me a camera and I was very excited to be taught how to use this valuable gift. My first picture was of the Shell building taken from Hungerford Bridge. I still have the print. It is a remarkably fine picture – I still think so!

Father's careful planning

Looking back with a more discerning eye and mature vantage point I begin to see how most aspects of our life were the result of careful planning by this quiet, self-effacing man, whether it was for his own social life or for his children's education and culture. He was always busy creating new, exciting activities. Even mealtimes were not to be wasted, when he was ready with a book of general knowledge questions.

The winter evenings were times to gather round the long dining room table to play Mahjong or Racing Demon. When grown-up guests were there we would play bridge with match sticks for money. Bumblepuppy was very popular too. We would play billiards or board games such as draughts, Lotto, and Snakes & Ladders. Sometimes my father would set up the magic lantern.

In summer the tennis court was carefully weeded and marked out. It was not only used for tennis as croquet was a favourite game. My father was able to banish other people's balls to the far corners of the lawn and in the process take his own ball through all the hoops in record time. Alternative games might be quoits or shuttlecock.

Bicycle riding

In the warm weather I had my own personal pastime. I would get on my bicycle and ride out to distant places pretending to be an Indian brave carrying important messages. I remember riding along the beautiful paths of Petts Wood and discovering a plaque on a tree telling the world that William Willet was the inventor of British Daylight Saving Time (Summer Time). In today's climate of fear it is truly remarkable to think that a small child of ten was able to go so far afield in perfect safety and confidence. It may seem amazing that my parents allowed me to wander so far away – but since I never thought of telling them it's a sure thing they didn't know!

Chislehurst caves

One adventure we never tired of was visiting the Chislehurst Caves. The entrance to these famous caves was just behind the livery stables that were my second home. Every visitor that came to see us was an excuse to explore the vast system of tunnels that spread beneath Chislehurst Common. At the entrance you were each given a little oil lantern and herded together to await your guide. On the way through the labyrinth of tunnels – endlessly crossing and intersecting each other – you were entertained by being shown fossils and the bones of an ancient mammoth monster.

Finally you came to a small opening in the wall where it was necessary to bend your head to enter. This was so that if you were an enemy your head could be struck off! "Now we must stay close together. There is no echo. If you got lost you would never be found!" In trepidation you were then led to the alter, the heart of the caves. At this moment the guide would disappear and take a hammer to something like a dustbin and an ear-splitting crash suddenly exploded into the air. Then you could hear echo after echo filling the tunnels with sound. Here, and only here, could echoes be heard. If, being lost, you found your way here you could be saved.

Father's influence

Taking part in all the games we played meant that I became more involved with the life of the family. There was the joy of achievement and the fun of competition. I then felt myself to be an active part of the group. Yet at the same time it brought me no nearer to my father. I can't remember any direct contact with him or speaking with him directly. Nor were we the kind of family that discussed together. Yet in some ways I followed in his footsteps. The books he read, I read: Jeffery Farnol, Dornford Yates' *Berry & Co*, P G Woodhouse, Zane Grey – he loved Westerns.

My father's manners were impeccable and he had the courage of his convictions. One felt that he had the highest standards of morality according to which he lived. This was the atmosphere we lived and breathed. Unconsciously we absorbed it. Looking back we can appreciate how painful it must have been when in our later lives we fell below the standards set in our formative years.

Felt a part of mother

With my mother it was quite different. Although she was no more of a hands-on person than my father, I always felt myself to be a part of her. She made our clothes and of course took us shopping for our needs. I remember she used to cut my hair and tried to make it curl for parties with big curling tongs. But there had always been nurses or governesses. After Ginger left there was a succession of Swedish au-pairs to looked after us.

From a tender age I noticed the clothes my mother wore and had strong mixed feelings when she cut short her long hair. I just loved to be near her, taking part in each new creative activity that her fancy focussed on. She had a special rose garden that needed constant attention and there was a special glass frame built against the wall of the house where she grew enormous mop-headed chrysanthemums. Of course there were always puppies tripping us up and getting into trouble.

From time to time the wonderful smell of apple jelly, marrow jam and green tomato chutney would come from the kitchen. Soon afterwards colourful jars would be admired on the shelves alongside bottled plums, gooseberries and other fruits in large

Kilner jars. Winter time was knitting time. Sitting by the fire we struggled over complicated patterns and designs while chestnuts popped on the open grate.

Mother's nervous exhaustion

But gradually we noticed that these activities slowed down. The enthusiasm began to wane and everything became a chore. My mother suffered from nervous exhaustion and she had to rest every afternoon between two and four, when we must be sure not to disturb her. "Hush, your mother is resting," became the cry.

Also we knew she mustn't be worried. One afternoon I nearly cut off my toe on a piece of glass lurking in the bed of the stream. Blood was colouring the water as I climbed up the bank and there was a trail behind me as I climbed the steps into the house. Bloody footsteps were left in the hall. When I was greeted by shrieks of dismay from the housemaid all I could gasp was, "Don't tell mummy!"

No more puppies appeared after George died so we were just left with Coo-ee and her daughter Sally. Entertaining became an exhausting duty for my mother that entailed a quick 'nip' in the pantry for sustenance.

It was at this time that Peggy went to boarding school and life changed.

Vegetarianism

I'm not sure when it began to dawn on me that there was a major difference between us and the people around us. Vegetarianism was for us a way of life. It was strange to us that people should eat the flesh of animals, chickens and other creatures that were killed and then cooked. It horrified us that people could be so insensitive, so lacking in feeling, that they could actually prepare and eat a baby calf that had been playing beside its mother in the fields not long before.

It seems that when they first met my parents were both troubled with health problems and they began practising a meat-free diet in order to cure the recurring illnesses that beset them. But having launched themselves onto this new regimen it very quickly turned into a crusade for animal welfare. The house became littered with literature describing the cruelty involved in farming and food production. Information concerning anti-vivisection, the International League for the Protection of Horses and other animal welfare societies regularly came by post. We had connections with the Blue Cross kennels situated on Shooters Hill, Blackheath, and in the evenings much of our time was spent making a variety of gifts to be sold at bazaars organised to raise money for animal charities.

Many people wondered how we remained alive on our restricted diet. They had no idea that by the Twenties a thriving industry of health foods and therapies was underway. We had our health food stores where we could buy not only nuts of every kind but also dried fruit, wholemeal flour, soft brown sugar and Nutter instead of lard. Several companies, such as PR (Physical Regeneration), Mapletons and Granose were making wonderfully tasty nutmeats that unfortunately are no longer available. A delicacy called Fruit & Nut Cake with a special filling was something to die for. Recipe books were also available. I have one in front of me now called *A Comprehensive Guide-Book to Natural, Hygienic and Humane Diet* by Sidney H Beard, first published in 1902. Many of the recipes in this book are still family favourites.

My mother suffered deeply as a result of her research into the incredible cruelty perpetrated on every kind of dumb animal for the benefit of human beings – each new revelation caused her more pain. She made sure that whenever possible she practised what she preached. We would wear fake fur and eschewed leather products. My father even had one of the first wire tennis rackets.

Peggy Pony

One bitter winter's day we were walking back from Elmstead station and passing a field heavily covered in snow when we suddenly saw a small pony standing miserably up to its shoulders in snow. This was a sight impossible to be ignored! My mother had no rest until she had discovered the owners and managed to rescue this scrap of misery. Luckily alongside our large garage, which had obviously been built to house a carriage or two, there was a stable with room for at least three horses. There was no difficulty in making a home for Peggy Pony, the little Shetland pony who became part of our family.

By this time old Mr and Mrs Mac, our former gardener and cook, had passed away. Now Mr Thrush looked after the garden, Dorothy Borkett was our cook and Violet Philips the maid of all work. Peggy was too small for us to ride so it became one of Violet's duties and joys to exercise Peggy, usually with one of the dogs riding on her back. Violet was a bit of a tom-boy who had been brought up by a strict father who thought nothing of taking the strap to her if the necessity arose. She was also well up to the task of grooming Peggy and mucking out her stable – with my able assistance!

British patriotism

Living in the early years of post-war Britain it was impossible not to be drawn into the web of patriotism and hatred of the 'Hun.' For my mother the only good German was a dead one. Some of the war propaganda was still current and believed. We had a paperback book illustrated in the manner of a children's comic and in it were pictures of near naked barbarians depicting in humorous style the antics and history of these Huns (for 'Huns' read 'Germans').

We had a contraption you looked through which brought photographs of the battlefield vividly to life.

There was a pride in being British and this centred on the Royal family. At the cinema and theatre everyone stood to attention when the national anthem was played. Not only were we British but we were also part of the British Commonwealth of Nations and the British Empire. Our Royal Navy patrolled the seas – Britannia ruled the waves!

We were never likely to forget that the Royal Navy was the senior service, looking down on the army as somewhat inferior. The fact that our father happened to be an officer in the navy gave us a special feeling of pride. His letters were addressed not to a mere 'Mr' but to 'Capt. A C Goolden CBE.' Whenever our behaviour became at all unseemly we were told: "Remember that you are daughters of an officer and a gentleman." Actually my father retired from the navy before the war began. His specialty was to do with guns and during the war he was co-opted onto the Ordnance Board. By the time I was conscious of such things he was superintendent of the Research Department at Woolwich, overseeing a group of scientists bent on discovering the most sophisticated means for men to kill each other.

Visit to the Research Department at Woolwich

The Research Department was situated within the premises of the Royal Arsenal at Woolwich. Once Peggy and I accompanied our father there on a Saturday morning. We passed through big iron gates and parked the car by rows of low buildings. As my father disappeared a young man took us in charge and, for our amusement, gave us a conducted tour of all the offices and workshops. There was a shed devoted to experiments with cordite where we had to make sure we had nothing metal about us and put on special slippers of enormous size made of felt. One spark, we were told, would send the whole building sky high.

Then there was a huge dark building where they demonstrated to us how lightening travelled. With a tremendous crackle and flash a streak of electricity flashed from one end of the shed to the other. We were then led to the office block where we found an old friend we called the 'Funny Man' who showed us some ice so cold that it smoked. From there we were escorted back to the car by our father. The caretaker presented us with a big bunch of flowers for my mother and we drove home with our heads full of the wonders we had beheld!

Father's colleagues visited socially

Several of the scientists working in the Research Department were my father's personal friends who came to our house on social occasions. The 'Funny Man' was Colonel Parcell, his wife, Tibs, we called the 'Kind Lady.' Perhaps it had something to do with the fact that she was manageress at Selfridges and brought us gifts from there. Alwyn Crow was another colleague who often came to visit. When he was with us it was an occasion to gather round the piano – a lovely grand that had originally belonged to him – and sing songs to his accompaniment. He had a collection of bawdy songs he would sing to us as well. One comes back to me where the words seem to be a love song and yet came out with such images such as, "When I see a comb without any teeth, I think of you dear!"

Beechbrook, Lubbock Road, Chislehurst

Other members of the Research Department were Godfrey Rotter, Robert Robertson, Mrs C Long, S Rees, N Pullen and H Pristen.

Beechbrook

Beechbrook

Beechbrook stables

Beechbrook garden flooded

Sunbury, 1929

Letchworth, 7 October 1928

Peggy and Pat - Beechbrook 1929

At the back are aunt Olive, uncle Dick and mother with cousins in the front

Pat on left, mother on far right

Peggy on left, Pat second from right

Pat and mother front, Alan and Peggy back

Pat and father on left

Birchington, 1926 – Pat in deck chair, Peggy standing

Swanage, 1928 - Peggy centre, Pat standing at back, mother with dog

Peggy in deck chair. Pat reading in caravan

Father in deck chair, Pat in caravan

Listening to gramophone

4

St Christopher School

1927 - 1931

The reason that St Christopher School in Letchworth was chosen by my parents is simple enough. It was the only vegetarian boarding school in England. Founded by Theosophists during the First World War in 1915, Chris was one of the few co-educational, progressive schools in existence in the 1920s. Others were Dartington Hall, Bedales and Frensham Heights, their ideas being well in advance of their time. The children were given a great deal of freedom – though not to the extreme extent as at Summer Hill run by A S Neil – and with that freedom came a certain amount of responsibility.

Many interesting people were attracted to St Christopher. Quite a few Quakers were to be found amongst the staff, Lyn Harris, the headmaster, being one of them. Here one became aware of a wider world of cultures and ideas. Suddenly the windows of one's mind were blown right open. Michael Winner's disparaging remarks about the school in the media are absolutely ridiculous and quite untrue. *[Michael Winner was an old scholar].*

Pat determined to go to St Chris

Certainly when Peggy returned home after her first term at Chris she was changed. It was difficult to put one's finger on just what that change consisted of, but my one and only aspiration from then onwards was to follow in her footsteps. That I was three years younger than her and only 12 years old made no difference to me. I gave my parents no peace until they gave way and agreed to let me go.

There was a question of a test to be taken before being accepted. I remember my father, a mathematician, attempting to teach me arithmetic (or was it algebra?) and losing his temper – something he very rarely did. This did nothing for my self-confidence. Apparently I was accepted, for my next memory is going to Bromley with my mother, clothes list in hand, to buy all the necessities required from Medhurst's department store. A big trunk appeared and began to be filled with all my possessions neatly packed away, name tags in place. Soon we were driving with both our parents in the big Humber car on our way to school.

Letchworth Garden City

Letchworth Garden City, where St Christopher School is situated, was the first of its kind. It was established in Hertfordshire in 1904 on six square miles of land 35 miles from London. The Garden City movement owes it origin to Ebenezer Howard's book *Tomorrow: a Peaceful Path to Social Reform* published in 1898. According to my *Harmsworth Universal Encyclopaedia* (1920) a garden city is "a town designed for healthy living and industry; of a size that makes possible a full measure of social life, but not larger; surrounded by a rural belt; the whole of the land being in public ownership, or held in trust for the community."

Hertfordshire is on the whole flat with a bracing wind that blows from the east. Entering this specially created town with its neat new individually architected houses, each set in a fair-sized garden, made you aware of a wind of change. Here the past had no place. Here was an exciting new development in the process of being created. This was the right place for a young school crammed with new ideals.

Arundale House

Arundale House, where we boarders lived, was a warm, purpose-built building with wood much in evidence. On the ground floor was a large reception area, the staff room, and the children's library (if I remember correctly). A swing door lead to the dining room, kitchen, larder, and cloakrooms. Then, further along, was a little room where we could have a party for birthday celebrations.

On the first floor were the boys' dormitories and the Harris's living quarters. There was also a wing comprising the surgery, dispensary, linen room, and practice rooms for music. Up another set of steep stairs and you came to the girls' dormitories. Going along a corridor you came to Hot Stuff and Little Hot Stuff where we younger ones slept.

Home-sickness

Possibly because my sister was there I somehow felt immediately at home, so it came as a surprise to find something very odd was happening to my throat. I couldn't swallow my food. It was such a worrying problem that I went to Sister at surgery time and reported ill. She was able to explain the trouble. "It's a case of home-sickness," I was told. She took me to the big linen cupboard and told me to climb up onto the top shelf and curl up in a nest of eiderdowns. This treatment worked and I remember thinking how odd it was that consciously I had no pangs but my body should have the symptoms.

Hot Stuff

We in Hot Stuff all got on together remarkably well. Mary Soutar, Dorothy Swan, Joan Hyde – and I think also Brenda Sayers – were the permanent group with others who came as temporary members. In Little Hotstuff I remember Billie Bennett, whose mother was a superb chocolate fudge maker, and also Nada Howard Flanders.

Life began after lights out and went on with only the occasional interruption until we fell exhausted into bed. Miss Elvis played fair. You could hear her tap-tapping heels on the lino floor of the corridor well in advance of her entrance, when we would all be tucked up in bed. But Sister wore slippers that gave no warning and she often surprised us during our activities.

Once Lyn Harris, standing in his rose garden far beneath us, summoned us down to stand before him in our slippers and dressing gowns. Our punishment was to run round the playing field, it being the summer term. Since it comprised the cricket pitch, the lacrosse pitch and two football pitches our excess energy was well and truly spent.

Getting up in the morning

In the morning there were three bells rung by a maid. The first was the wake-up bell which gave us good time to get out of bed, wash and dress before the first breakfast bell. The third bell was the final summons and you had to be standing behind your chair in the dining room before it finished ringing. Some people had great difficulty in getting out of bed in the morning and the poor maid would carry on ringing while there were clattering sounds of footsteps on the stairs and bodies streaking past her. On one occasion Phyllis Dax had to be forcibly restrained from hurtling down stairs without a stitch on. Dennis Coombes was so often late that he ate many a meal standing by the mantelpiece.

Main school

The main school was, to my inexperienced eyes, a very impressive building. Since Barry Parker had been one of the main architects of

Letchworth, I assume that his hand had also been involved in the creation of the school buildings. As far as I can remember the classrooms were arranged around a central quadrangle. Two or three of these faced onto a lawn on their outer side and had huge doors the width of the room which could be opened to form extra study space on the veranda. The library was at the far end and, with a little practice, it was possible to sneak round the doors – if the lesson got at all boring – and escape into it for a little light relief!

There was a big hall for gym and eurhythmics and, wonder of wonders, a big theatre! How amazed was I to see Peter Young and Geoffrey Parker, boys from the top class, playing cricket in the aisles – it was mind boggling! It was one of my first impressions of the school.

Company adviser

There were many things to get used to in this new environment. Since each child had his/her own timetable there were no recognisable class groups so we were divided into companies. Each company had an adviser. When we arrived at school in the morning we didn't go to 'our classroom' but met together with our adviser. He or she was the person you could approach with any question or problem as it arose. At first my company adviser was James Potter, a tall man with a cast in one eye. He was very kind and caring – but I wanted to belong to the Gym Company that did gym every morning before school! It took me some time, but finally the day came when I was admitted.

Teachers

We had a different teacher for each subject and went to the class that would cater for our abilities. For maths we were taught by Mr Cuckoo, a small choleric man whose main ability was to take unerring aim with a piece of chalk, striking an inattentive pupil with great accuracy. Miss Hargreaves ruled over our domestic science studies, teaching us the mysteries of cooking. My sister Peggy had gained a reputation for rather unruly behaviour so Miss Hargreaves took no chances with me. As soon as I appeared to indulge in private conversation I found myself outside of the room. Mr Little was our French teacher, a gentle giant who had no idea of how to handle young children.

Accident

But my days in this enchanting new life were numbered. Not long after the beginning of term I was taking part in a gym lesson in the large hall and our gym teacher, Elsie Brooks, was swinging a rope round in a circle with a weight tied to the end. We were jumping over the rope when I tripped and fell heavily. My foot was extremely painful and the next morning, when it was realised that I wasn't making a fuss about nothing, I was taken to the cottage hospital. It was discovered that there was a broken bone and torn ligaments so the whole foot had to be encased in plaster. Since I was unable to put any weight on my foot and normal life was impossible I was sent home to recuperate.

My return home turned out to be an extreme embarrassment. My parents had decided that their new found freedom needed a celebration and had arranged to attend a caravan meeting. So after moving my bed into the downstairs study and hiring a wheelchair they departed, leaving me in the care of Dorothy and Violet. Dorothy, the cook, 'lived in' but Violet, who lived with her parents, came every day. She it was who looked after me and saw that I didn't die of boredom. She was quite inventive in thinking up amusements. Our most delightful escapade was charging round the garden, Violet pushing me at top speed in the wheelchair. Unfortunately this was brought to an abrupt end when an encounter with a rock in the vegetable garden sent me catapulting out of the chair – luckily landing on my good leg.

End of childhood

It was a strange experience living in the big house without my parents, my only companions two working class girls, one still in her teens. We got on very well together. They were my friends. This time marked the end of my childhood.

Town Court Cottage, Petts Wood

Eventually I went back to school and finished the term. Coming back for the holidays was the beginning of a new life. While we were away my parents had moved to a new home, Town Court Cottage in Petts Wood, which was really two cottages made into one. It was a poky little place compared to Beechbrook. Peggy Pony had gone to a home for old horses, the Dumb Friends League. I never saw my train set or farm animals again. A room for Peggy had to be built over the coal hole. Only the grand piano remained as a memory of former days.

My parents' life adjusted to the new circumstances. Help was forthcoming in the shape of Milly, the maid of all work. Gone were the spacious kitchen, pantry and scullery. A pint-sized little room with nothing but a gas stove proved capable of producing three meals a day – with the odd coffee or tea thrown in for good measure. There was a bucket in the corner for the eggs in winter where they were submerged in an unappetising liquid to preserve them. Shelves were weighed down with endless bottles of marrow jam, apple jelly and green tomato chutney, not to mention Kilner jars full of gooseberries, plums and rhubarb. The kitchen proper was more like a passageway. One end was occupied by a boiler, a dresser ran along one wall, and by the window was a table with chairs. That left just enough room for the dog baskets. When we moved from Beechrook we were down to one little bitch, Sally, the last puppy that was left from the last litter Coo-ee ever had before she died. The dogs were fed on a vegetarian diet and Sally didn't really thrive on this. She was nervy and even a bit neurotic, but she was the family dog and the other animals who arrived later were not allowed to forget it.

Widdee-Woo and Popsy

In order to explain the increase from one to two dogs again we have to include Peggy in the picture. She, being something of a stunner, naturally attracted members of the opposite sex. Already at Beechrook she had had a boyfriend who came to stay. Alan Young was a nice young man but he was only around for a while before Geoffrey Parker took his place. For some time the two of them were very close, but when this friendship came to an end, by way of a parting gift, Geoffrey gave her a puppy. Widdee-woo was a long-haired, witless, excitable dog that never stood still. When Peggy left, Widdee-Woo stayed.

And then there was Popsy, the stray. I always felt sorry for Popsy. She was never allowed to forget that she was not a member of the family. She was more of a smooth-haired fox terrier than anything else. She had large, mournful eyes and a tentative, nervous air. She was grateful for anything she received, never put a foot wrong, and knew that her place was at the back of the queue. It reminded me a little that I too, as the younger daughter, had my place in the pecking order.

Broadway building sold

It must have been about a year after I arrived at Chris that the magnificent buildings on Broadway were sold to a convent and the new buildings attached to Arundale were ready for occupation. It was sad saying goodbye to all the amenities of the grand old school, but the new arrangement had its advantages. At least it was pleasant in winter to be able to reach our classrooms under cover, no longer trekking in all weathers from Barrington Road to the Broadway and back every day.

Freedom

St Christopher was known as a progressive school which meant that the children had a great deal of freedom. For a dreamy child like me the freedom was intoxicating.

Sport and art

I have enduring memories of life at school but the content of the lessons does not form part of them. Games played a large part in my life. Tennis, netball and lacrosse were all entered into with enthusiasm. The school had just changed from playing hockey to lacrosse, which had been our main game at my previous school, so I began with a considerable advantage in the early stages of the charge-over.

Emphasis was given to art and craft in the curriculum, and the art and woodwork rooms always remained open. We were free to spend any spare time we liked in either place.

Drama

In those days drama did not play a significant role in our education, but an unforgettable part of the school's history must be the occasion when *Trial by Jury* was performed by the staff with the children making up the chorus. It was a resounding success and enjoyed by everybody. Mr Ferrybough was the Judge, Mr Cuckoo the Defendant, Dorothy Sergeant the Plaintiff, and Mr Little the Usher. I can still sing large chunks of it from memory.

Dance

Dancing was one of my favourite pastimes. Elsie Brooks taught us ballroom dancing but some of us, particularly Shanta Bignold and I, spent many hours perfecting our skills to the music of my portable gramophone. We also learnt Dalcroze eurhythmics with Nora Knaggs and natural movement with Winifred Swan. When I left school I continued having lessons with her and also performed with her. She became quite famous and performed on television.

Debate

One important event stands out in my memory. Being the year of the general election it was decided that the school should hold its own private election. David Barker was the Conservative candidate, but there was no one interested in standing as a Labour candidate. I was totally dumbfounded when David came to ask me if I would volunteer. Having no knowledge of party politics and no idea of what I was letting myself in for, in all ignorance I agreed to take on the job. By the end of a week of diligent study of all the leaflets and brochures I became a rabid socialist. At my first 'public' meeting, when David Baker attempted to tear me to shreds, my newfound fanatical enthusiasm for my cause won over many converts and brought David to a standstill. When it came to voting day I succeeded beyond my wildest dreams and lost by the narrowest of margins.

Going out with an older boy

It was about this time of my life when a complete change came about in my relationship with the opposite sex. Whereas boys had always regarded me as being 'not bad for a girl' and 'a good sort,' now I quite suddenly gained an attraction for them. They would offer to escort me to my hostel at bedtime and there was competition to partner me on the dance floor. All this was exciting and enjoyable, but also rather frightening. Any attempts made to engage me in closer friendships or relationships were not encouraged. I remained aloof and unattached – but also, I fear, something of a flirt!

All this was to change when one of the older boys, at least six years older than me, began an obsessive pursuit of me. This was the beginning of a nightmare that was to last for years. He was, or seemed to me, very sophisticated and self-assured. He had a first-class brain and yet he was also a very accomplished sportsman. Like a rabbit, I was fearful and yet fascinated. Even after leaving school and going up to Cambridge he continued the chase. He became so persistent that he was banned from the school grounds. The crunch came when, disregarding the ban, he persuaded me to go out for a ride in his car one evening. Then, finding his watch had stopped, he dumped me back at school well after 'lights out.' It was decided that it was time for me to leave school and pursue my further education abroad.

Gym Company flattens out the cricket pitch, 1931

Pat second from right

Bournemouth hockey tournament

Joy and Phyllis on left, Pat on far right

Hinchcliff 1928 – Rosemary, Joy, Pat, Dorothy Swan (front), Joan Nicholson, Audrey Gibson right

St. Christopher School, Letchworth.
Mathematical Group.

St. Christopher School, Letchworth.
Art Shop

St. Christopher School, Letchworth.
Pupils at individual work on verandah.

Arundale House, St Christopher School

5

Lausanne

1931 - 1932

I left school without anything to show for my education except passes at Grade 8 for the violin and piano. After the fiasco occasioned by the older boy, Peter Young, my parents were keen to send me abroad, preferably to a finishing school in Switzerland. My thoughts turned to continuing with my music so it was finally decided that I should attend a college of music in Lausanne. The Minister for Education himself made all the arrangements for us. We met his daughter, Mini, who happened to be staying in England at the time, and all was in order for me to go. I would be staying in their pensionat in Lausanne.

At last, with a brave face and sinking feeling in the pit of my stomach, I sat in the overnight train to Switzerland. Paris was a nightmare. We spent the night being shunted backwards and forwards under harsh, cold lights accompanied by the shouting of foreign voices. I was convinced that my carriage would soon be travelling to Moscow or some other far distant destination. It wasn't until we arrived at Lausanne that my doubts were dispelled.

I was welcomed into the Rees household, which occupied a large apartment in Avenue Tissot. There was the Rees family itself comprising M. and Mme Rees, Mini, Bichette, Renée, a son who was at university, and a little terrier known as Kitty. In addition there was not only me but 'The Professor,' M. Golay, and five other students. There was Alvaro Bwimester Martius da Costa, a very aristocratic Spaniard, Gilbert, who was German, Peter Bodenhorn of the Floris scent family, and two non-descripts who shared a room and continually fought.

LAUSANNE

Apart from attending the music college I also went to the École des Étrangers to learn French and German. This was a case of entering the real world. At sixteen I found it enlightening, intoxicating and frightening by turns. It was pleasant to discover that when the students (male) raised their white caps to you, this was a compliment of high order. A visit to the centre of town revealed the delights of its many patisseries. There was an endless variety of wonderful biscuits and cakes which were beyond description!

In winter we went skiing in the mountains and skating, then in summer we went swimming and boating. I received three proposals of marriage, learnt a lot about men, and, by the time I came home, Peter Young had become my boyfriend.

My piano teacher was really nice. She introduced me to another English girl living in Lausanne with her mother – a strange eccentric pair who seemed to belong to another century. But we got on well together studying a Mendelssohn concerto for two pianos. My violin teacher, who played in the Lausanne Orchestra, was not so nice.

My great love had always been the violin. I was not allowed to learn the instrument until I went to boarding school, so when it was finally possible to have lessons they were entered into with dedication and enthusiasm. My playing was on a par with my piano skills in record time. But in Switzerland my violin teacher was soon picking holes in my musical knowledge, which was pretty basic, and discovered my complete ignorance of the theory of harmony and composition. She gave me a very hard time and my self-confidence, never great at any time, was completely crushed. Added to this my shoulder became very painful with an attack of fibrositis. It seemed to me that my hopes of a musical career were at an end. I decided to call it a day.

With love from.
[signature]

RADA

1932 - 1934

Because she had had a secret longing to be an actress, my mother was eager for me to follow an acting career. Having no other ideas in mind I agreed to 'have a go.' We applied to the Royal Academy of Dramatic Art and they suggested a coach who could prepare me for the audition. Surprisingly – to some people – I sailed through the audition and was admitted. Ten students were chosen out of two hundred odd, so it was remarkable that I was chosen after so little preparation.

I soon got used to the daily train journey from Petts Wood to central London and was much in awe of my fellow class mates, all older, sophisticated and worldly people.

The work was fascinating. We had several really good teachers, including some well-known actors and actresses such as Dorothy Green, Sara Allgood, Mme Gashet (who had been a member of the French Comedie Français), and Irene and Violet Vanburgh.

My mind was opened to Shakespeare and Chaucer on the one hand, and Noel coward and Bernard Shaw on the other. This was a world I could escape into, away from the problems brought by Peter Young – who had of course entered my life once again! He was in London training to be a Lyons Tea Shop manager and, as always, created mayhem both in my studies and my private life.

Life at RADA was well ordered and disciplined, with lessons in voice production, fencing and ballet. We also had to prepare for the performances of about three plays a term. These included a Shakespeare, a Greek or Chaucer, and a modern play. They could be performed in either the Little Theatre or the Big Theatre. I was chosen to take part in a French play to be performed in the Public

RADA

Theatre. This happened only every other year so I was very excited. Then I found that the man playing opposite me had been replaced by someone else. Unfortunately we were completely incompatible and our time was removed. I cried buckets!

Students at RADA at the same time as Pat included Trevor Howard, Margaret Lockwood and Howard Marion-Crawford.

TELEPHONE: MUSEUM 7076.

ROYAL ACADEMY OF DRAMATIC ART.

62-64, GOWER STREET,

W.C.1.

20th. April, 1937.

To all whom it may concern:

    Miss Patricia Goolden, who is now Mrs. Pat Young, took a course at the R.A.D.A. of two years - 1932 to 1934 - and was awarded a Certificate of Merit.

    During her studentship she applied herself to the studies with commendable thoroughness, and her general character was in every way satisfactory; had this not been the case she would not have been awarded a Certificate of Merit.

Kenneth R. Barnes.

Principal.

7

THE OLD THATCHED BARN, TENTERDEN

1935

My lack of confidence and naivety prevented me from even beginning to seek a job on the stage, so it was no wonder that I became embroiled in the schemes of Peter Young. I don't think he ever finished the manager's course, but somehow persuaded his father to put up the money to buy a roadhouse.

We finally found just what we were looking for, the Old Thatched Barn near Tenterden. It sat beside a main road which soon divided, one branch leading to Ashford and the other to Maidstone, promising plenty of traffic passing our doors. In high hopes we set out on our adventure with a lady cake maker as chaperone and Mills, the young boy who worked in the garden. We also had Binnie the bull-terrier and a resident cat.

We were kept satisfactorily busy and I was becoming overwhelmed serving teas. Then one day in Tenterden we saw a young man at the side of the footpath selling matches. He was quite illiterate but presentable, so we put him in a white coat and taught him how to lay and clear tables – and even take orders. In our spare time I was teaching him to read and write.

Deciding that Binnie should have a mate we visited some local kennels that bred bull-terriers. But instead of choosing a suitable dog we were overcome with pity when we saw a young white male sitting all by himself. After being told he was deaf and useless for breeding we found it impossible to leave him there. Puck then became one of the family.

Binnie was a very good mother, she even took charge of the

litter of kittens on their arrival and attended to their ablutions, up-ending them on every occasion.

It was not long before our chaperone decided that Tenterden was too far from Ashford and her boyfriend and give in her notice. This created a crisis of a domestic nature.

My parents, however, gave their permission for our marriage, it being preferable to the thought of us living together in sin. By this time I felt very uncertain and had grave doubts about my feelings. Peter's temper, never much under control, had not improved with time. I was too young and naïve to be able to combat his vitriolic attacks and this had a destructive effect on my self-confidence. Yet it seemed too late, now, to draw back. It seemed that I had burnt all my boats behind me. Probably my meek inability to stand up for myself fired his anger all the more.

There were good times as well as bad, but the winter saw the end of our passing trade. We started a home-made cake business and I was called upon to visit houses with a selection of cakes in the back of the car, sometimes finding myself stuck along lonely cart tracks. But it was a losing battle and there came a time when we had to face the fact that we hadn't the funds to live through another winter.

We managed to sell the Barn for a good price, but of course all the money went straight back to the long-suffering 'Daddus.' We were left homeless and penniless.

Mother seated next to Pat

Peter Young with Binnie

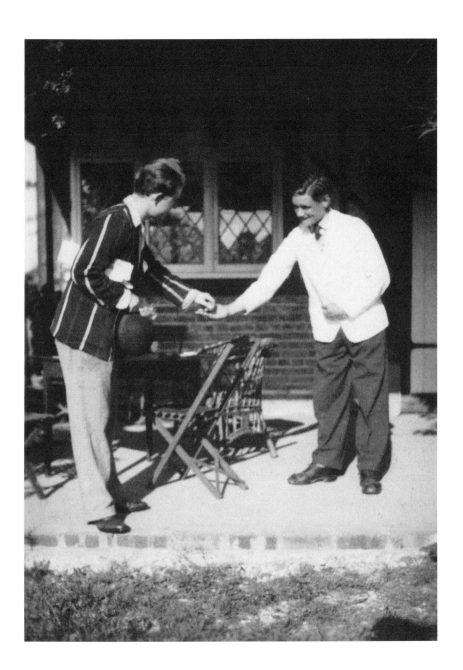

8

RESCUED FROM ADDISCOMBE

The next few months remain dim, dark, bleak memories of struggling to survive, moving from one impossible situation to another. Was it in Addiscombe that we finally settled in a ghastly flat? It was ugly and dirty beyond description! Why we were there and what we were doing there I have no idea.

I have a vague picture of falling ill, of my parents' sudden appearance, and then being lifted into their car and driven home. It took me quite a while to recover my health and strength. In all that time there had been no word from Peter. Once I travelled over to the flat, but he was not there. What I did find on the windowsill was a dainty lace handkerchief.

This was a shock to my system. No use waiting for his return or leaving a note. The only thing to be done was to return to my parents in despair.

9

BERLIN

1937

It was not to be the end of my marriage after all. Peter came to tell me that he had been offered a job in a Jewish school in Berlin, but to accept this teaching post in a girls school he needed to be married. Would I come? Naturally I was sceptical and questioning about possible relationships with the opposite sex. He was adamant that there was no female involvement, so I finally agreed to accompany him to Germany.

The school was situated in one of the really high class districts of Berlin. We were given a room in a beautiful house, the rent for which took practically all Peter's salary. My memory of our time there is very vague because we stayed such a short time. I remember that somehow we managed to bring with us our brindle bull-terrier, Binnie, which now seems to me quite remarkable.

What I clearly remember is the atmosphere of fear, which was quite palpable, that spread throughout this Jewish community. We were in the mid-1930s when Hitler's Nazis were beginning their persecution of the Jews. Dr Goldstein, the owner of this school for Jewish girls, was without doubt a remarkably courageous woman in the way she stood up to the intimidation and bullying meted out by Nazi officialdom. Her husband was a lawyer who was able to make sure she never infringed or broke the law in any way and she continued to walk a very dangerous tightrope in keeping her school open.

As Peter became more involved in school affairs I was left in something of a vacuum. I remember meeting some of the girls in the nearby hostel. They talked in subdued voices about their situation and there was obviously a great deal of nervous tension.

Another memory is of one of my daily walks with Binnie when we were accosted by a burly policeman. He shouted at me in German – not a world of which I understood – while pointing to the dog. It was clear that he was intent of taking us to the police station. I was absolutely petrified and feared the worst. At the station I was able to make them understand where I came from. After an anxious wait help appeared and we were rescued. Our crime turned out to have been that our dog did not possess a name tag.

My next shock was more of a body blow. We had just settled down into a recognisable routine when Peter suddenly informed me that he could not stay in Germany any longer. He had to return to England, back to some girl he had met who worked in a shoe shop. Heartbroken and humiliated, all I could say when called to an interview at the school was that I had no influence over my husband, that there was no possibility I could persuade him to change his mind.

We returned to England. Binnie was put into the Blue Cross kennels to spend her six months quarantine in exile, and Peter and I went our separate ways.

WIFE

BRITISH CONSULATE G...

PHOTOGR... OF BEARER

BERLIN

BRITISH CONSULATE GENERAL

A FEMME.

**

K. P. Young.

10

CHIROPODY

1937 - 1938

Finding a new direction for my life proved easier than anticipated. My self-confidence was by now shot to pieces so there was no possibility of thinking of the stage. Also, my insight into the superficial life that actors and actresses seemed to lead had turned me against being a part of that scene. Having very little money in the bank, I trawled through magazines and newspapers looking for some kind of training which would be provision for the future. I found one course my small savings would cover. I applied and was accepted.

Soon I found myself a student of the Westminster School of Chiropody. Mother Lilian, my kind mother-in-law, supplied me with a smart, white coat and Daddus agreed to give me an allowance to top up the £3 per week I received from my parents. Soon I found myself in a dismal bedsit in Belsize Park for the princely sum of 10s per week. There was just enough room for the bed and for me to stand beside it. The window looked out onto a blank brick wall.

Breakfast mostly consisted of half a grapefruit, a slice of toast, and tea. As it usually turned out to be my main meal of the day there was no chance of my becoming obese. For lunch I could choose between a bowl of soup with a roll at the local Lyons Corner House or a packet of ten cigarettes. They each cost six pence.

The chiropody course lasted a year and proved interesting. There was a great deal to learn and it was a real slog, which is just what I needed! I remember that as a passing out gift Daddus gave me a beautiful leather instrument case.

I took the first job that offered, which was in a Lewisham foot clinic. The clients were mostly old, over-weight, working class women who spent their working lives on their feet – judging from the amount of callous we removed! There was an all-pervading smell of a mixture of methylated spirits – used rather than the more expensive alcohol to prepare for treatment – and stale sweat from the clients' feet. There were four of us working in open cubicles in a run-down, shabby clinic. Our team consisted of a middle-aged husband and wife, their daughter, a young man and myself. We were situated in the middle of town and were kept pretty busy from morning till evening.

I departed from my shoebox bedsit with a sigh of relief and determined that, come what may, I would never to subject myself to such a depressing experience again. I decided to take a big room with a kitchen in a quiet, middle-class neighbourhood. The street was lined with well-built, detached houses. The only drawback was that at 18s a week it swallowed up most of my salary. The magnificent feeling of space and the view from the windows of a well-ordered garden was balm to my soul! There was a gas stove in the kitchen and before I left for work in the morning I would put a potato to bake on a low gas. This would be ready and waiting to be eaten with salad on my return.

Some sort of social life began to emerge, but not of an entirely favourable kind. It soon became apparent that although there was no shortage of men, they were of the type attracted to an unattached married girl – considered an easy conquest!

I joined a tap-dancing class and found myself surrounded by a group of children half my size. It was pure joy to be dancing again! There came the time when we put on a performance and my sewing skills were brought into play when a sailor costume was needed.

It was during the first winter of working as a chiropodist, earning a living for the first time in my life, that I developed a hacking cough and pains in my chest. It showed no signs of moving with the warmer weather and became so bad that it seemed sensible to pay a visit to a doctor. He was not at all encouraging and told me that there was a danger of my becoming consumptive unless I could escape the rigours of another winter.

M.W.I.Ch.

DIPLOMA

OF

THE WESTMINSTER INSTITUTE OF CHIROPODY

awarded to *Katherine P. Young*

who has passed the Qualifying Examinations of this Institute, obtaining Distinctions in Theoretical, Clinical and Practical Chiropody, including Pedicure.

Granted Membership of The Westminster Institute of Chiropody this day the 3rd of September 1937.

V. Noel Surtees *Principal* | Signed | *Secretary* S. Day.

L.J. Ferguson M.D. B.Sc | Signed | *President*

The

WESTMINSTER CHIROPODISTS' ASSOCIATION

Diploma   No. 17.

This is to certify that

Katherine P. Young

was admitted a _Member_ of the
Association on the 13th day of October 1938.

Given under the Common Seal of
The Westminster Chiropodists' Association
London this 15th day of October 1938.

President.   Vice-President.   Secretary.

11

SOUTH AFRICA

1938 - 1939

When they heard this depressing news my parents once more came to my rescue with a proposition that was so utterly amazing that it was well beyond my wildest dreams. It all hinged on the fact that my sister had married a tea planter from Ceylon and was living with her husband, Tommy, on a plantation up in the hills in a place called Hindagala. She was now pregnant with their first child and my parents planned to go out and spend some time with her to give support while she was awaiting the birth.

Their suggestion was that I would travel with them as far as the Cape, where my uncle Dick and aunt Olive were living in Cape Town. I could stay there for a few months and then travel on to Ceylon and stay with Peggy for a while to help with the new baby. So it came about that we set sail one autumn morning on one of the big mail boats that sail from England to Australia and back.

To travel as a first class passenger on one of these enormous Castle ships was to live in the height of luxury. One's every wish was anticipated – superb food and drinks in the opulent dining room or bar, deck games and a swimming pool for one's entertainment, and dancing in the ballroom at night. All around was the vast expanse of an ever-changing sea.

I made friends with other young people on board and joined in the social life of the passengers. But nothing could remove my inner feeling of black despair and total lack of confidence that had lived with me as though for ever. This closed me off from any feeling of belonging, of being a part of the life around me. We were on the high seas for three weeks, calling in at Tenerife and St Helena on our way. My aunt and uncle met us on our arrival at Cape Town docks, where I disembarked.

It was easy to enter into the life I found in uncle Dick and aunt Olive's household. For many years my uncle had been the science teacher at Bishops, the English public school in Rondebosch, Cape Town, and they were both very much a part of the social set that the English residents had created there. The English way of life seemed to dominate the townships whereas the Afrikaner people were the farmers living on the land. In the slums and reserves in various states of poverty were the blacks, who made up the workforce for the white people. Many coloured people with some education worked in offices and shops, and there was a large population of Indian nationality.

Dick and Olive employed a black girl as a maid-of-all-work. I was quite shocked to find that she slept in a room built on the outside of the house so that she was locked out during the night. This, I later learnt, was the general practice for domestic servants throughout the area.

Jack and Peter were my two cousins. Jack was at university studying to equip himself to work on the game reserves and was learning to speak the native languages. Peter was still at school. This meant that Olive and I were thrown together quite a lot. This was fortunate for me because she was very fond of music. She was friends with the school music master, which meant that we were able to become members of the school orchestra. It was good to be able to play the violin again!

Olive had a vast collection of records and we had musical afternoons when friends would be invited to attend. One of her favourite composers was Elgar. It was a great joy to become familiar with the Enigma Variations and the Dream of Gerontius as well as his symphonies and concertos. There were also works by Bach, Beethoven and many others.

My uncle was a very sociable man and made many friends, some of them well-to-do with houses right by the sea. We were able to spend time in one of these.

The highlight of my whole visit was a camping trip to a dried up river bed by the sea at Rooi-Els. A long sandy beach was home to a flock of flamingos and a rocky outcrop nearby turned out to be the favourite haunt of a troupe of baboons. Sheer heaven!

It was not long after I arrived in South Africa that Christmas was upon us. In spite of it being the hottest time of the year in this region we were invited to a festive lunch with all the trimmings associated with Christmas in England. We then, if I remember rightly, went out to play tennis so full that it was difficult to move. In the evening a party of us went down to a sandy beach and pelted each other with slices of water melon.

A different kind of event must be recorded for posterity. It was a special day in commemoration of the history of South Africa and there was to be a meeting at the summit of Table Mountain. Many people were to be seen climbing up when we overtook an upright figure and stopped to talk. Who should it be but General Smuts, no less! And so it came about that I was introduced to and talked with this legendary figure.

Aunt Olive, mother, Pat and uncle Dick (front), cousins Jack and Peter (back)

3 December 1938 - Pat pulling rope, dressed in black

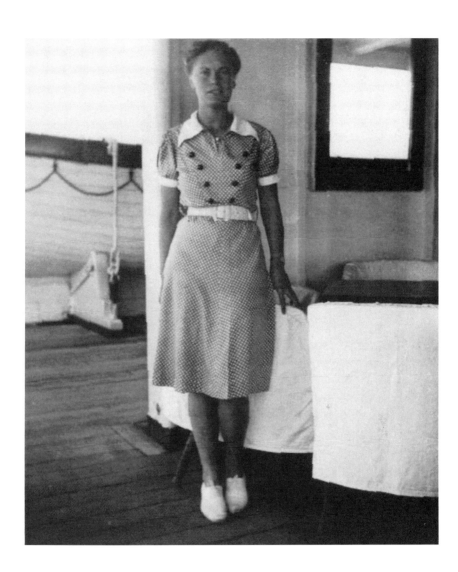

Mother in deck chair with Pat

UNION-CASTLE LINE TO SOUTH AND EAST AFRICA.

MOTOR VESSEL "DUNNOTTAR CASTLE." 15,007 TONS.

Uncle's house – Lynwood, Heseldon Road, Rondebosch, Cape Town

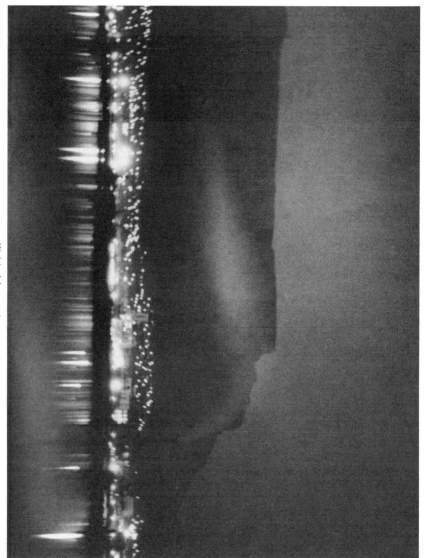

Table Mountain

Cape Town Port

12

CEYLON

1939

When the time came to leave and continue on my journey to Ceylon I found I had been booked a berth on a small, gleaming white ship called the Inchanga. The only other passengers on board were Billy and Lorna Frater, with whom I struck up a close friendship as we sailed up the east coast of Africa. This stood me in good stead during the war when rationing in England was strict and our diet limited. These friends living in southern Africa sent me very welcome parcels full of good things.

The ship was never far from land on her way up the coast but we only stopped at three ports: Dares Salaam, Zanzibar, and finally Mombasa. My parents, travelling in the sister ship to the Inchanga, had made friends with a lady who was a librarian in the locality Zanzibar port and she invited me to dinner on the night of our arrival. It was a very frightening test of my nerves to go out at night, alone, in a boat surrounded by dark men who looked alien and forbidding. Somehow I got to the lady's house, which seemed to have as many plants growing inside as out. I was so nervous that she must have thought I had lost my wits. Never was I more glad to find myself back in the security of my cabin!

There was another passenger on board who particularly came to my notice when we arrived at Mombasa. After the ship had been securely berthed our attention was drawn to a smart car that was being lowered by crane onto the dock below. This man was fully engaged in the operation, but it was what happened next that set my hackles rising. A black policeman appeared on the scene. He was attempting to lay down the law, which the owner of the car was in some way infringing, but the white man dismissed this representative of the law in a most high-handed manner. He used bad language that I found truly offensive. I surprised myself later that evening by accepting his invitation to go ashore for dinner in an extremely smart hotel.

All went well until we were driving back to the ship only to discover that it was gone. I couldn't believe my eyes! The thought of being stranded in Africa with not a penny in my purse gave me a real panic attack. It quickly passed, but already in that short time some very unladylike words had passed my lips – enough to shock a man unused to hearing the kind of language learnt at my old school, St Christopher. I was restored to perfect calm on espying my ship, which had been moved to another berth on the other side of the docks. It was a very frosty drive that took us to the ship's side. It was an even frostier goodbye as we parted and I thankfully climbed back on board.

Since saying goodbye to the slums of Lewisham my life had changed quite drastically for the better. Suddenly pressure of work, financial worries and the various unsolvable problems that life had presented all seemed to disappear. The little money that I had at my disposal was sufficient for my needs. I was floating with the tide, content to drift on the current that others had created for me. After the nightmare years I was encompassed by a different kind of dream. I drifted on until my little ship deposited me on the island of Ceylon.

Here was a new world! Living with my aunt and uncle in Rondebosch on the outskirts of Cape Town is to be surrounded by white people, mostly English. Apart from the coloured girl who worked for my aunt I was not conscious of encountering any black people. This was except for the one occasion I went with my aunt to help in a soup kitchen distributing soup and rolls to the poor blacks from a particular locality. But in Colombo one steps into the East, one is surrounded by brown skins, strange clothing and strange smells. It is a different, exciting world!

On arriving in Colombo I was first taken to the Galle Face Hotel for coffee before being whisked up to the tea plantation where my sister Peggy and her husband Tommy lived.

All I knew about the island was that it had been the happy hunting ground for various member of my extended family. As far as the story goes, Bob Coomb, an influential island-dweller, had been detailed to keep an eye on my wayward aunt Dorothy on her voyage out to visit relatives and ended up marrying her. They lived on a tea plantation in Poonagala where they raised their family of three children, Rosemary, John and Dick. My uncle Cyril and his wife Tinny lived on another plantation in Nuwara Eliya, raising their two children there, Marjory and Douglas. By the time Peggy married Tommy, Marjory was living in Colombo with her husband, a brother of the well-known actor Dickie Murdoch, and Rosemary was also married and living in Colombo.

It was a strange experience to see how the middle class English were continuing to live this comfortable existence underpinned by numerous servants and workers. But if one looked beneath the surface and kept an ear to the ground it was possible to hear the stirrings of unrest. The Tamils, I was told, made up the main workforce for the tea planters, being more hardworking and active than the Singhalese. For this reason more of them had been brought in from Southern India. There has always been trouble between the two races and this seems to have added to the resentment among the Tamils, who felt the need to improve their conditions and establish their rights.

I was staying with Peggy and Tommy on the Hindagala tea plantation where Tommy was manager. It was peaceful and pleasant. Their home was a modern, well-built bungalow. It was all was run very smoothly, there being a boy who cooked in a kitchen I never investigated and another boy who seemed to cover every other aspect of the work. There was also a gardener who watered the plants.

Down in the valley was the factory, which I visited with much interest. All was neat, clean and well organised. The cheapest tea was the sweepings from the factory floor – though I may be mistaken in this observation – but certainly the dried leaves were sifted through different sieves to be graded according to their size and then packed in wooden tea chests.

This journey seemed to be a return to my middle class roots after the hard grind and feelings of hopelessness I had experienced in the days of the world depression of the Thirties. After Cape Town, now there was the social round in Ceylon. It was a return – but I was not seeing with the same eyes as before. It was not so easy to find my place in this life again.

Any hopes I may have had of meeting any Singhalese or Tamil people were quickly extinguished. Once, at my request, we invited a couple for drinks at the club – but there was no opportunity to get to know them. My only memory of that evening was of Tommy and some of his friends amusing themselves by soaking bread in alcohol, tossing it to the crows, and watching their tipsy efforts to fly.

The social life revolved around the club. A little corner of England spread out and anchored itself to this strange land. Tennis, bridge and four o'clock tea held the English way of life firmly in place.

As my sister was pregnant with her first child it was arranged that Tommy should take me to a dance at a club some way down the road. Once we had arrived he disappeared to spend the evening propping up the bar. By closing time he was well and truly plastered.

On one side of the road a hill rose up steeply and disappeared into the darkness above. On the other side the bank dropped sharply into the valley below. Our road snaked around the hills, eerily lit by our headlamps. Tommy followed a weaving path from one side to the other, and luckily we fetched up on a culvert. My offer to drive was rejected. After a pause we continued safely home.

As I was trying to come to an understanding of all this the world scene broke in on our lives with dramatic effect. War was declared between England and Germany and I found myself on a ship bound for England. No way was it possible for me to sit out a war on a tiny island in the Indian Ocean. This was to be no pleasure cruise. We were held up for ten scorching days at Port Suez while the Admiralty decided whether it was safe to go through the Mediterranean. If Italy came into the conflict then we would have to return via the Cape.

Because blackout was enforced our cabins became unbearably hot and our request to sleep on deck was refused. Day after day we waited for the word. At last permission was given to proceed through the Med. Deck games became hazardous as our ship tacked from side to side to avoid torpedoes. At night we crept through the darkness, not a light to betray us. Only once were we challenged. When our captain refused to declare us a shot was sent across our bows as a warning – luckily by a Royal Navy gunboat. After three weeks of discomfort it was with feelings of great relief that we arrived in Liverpool.

I arrived unexpectedly at my parents' house as it had seemed better to keep them in ignorance of my somewhat hazardous journey home through enemy waters. I came to find my family preparing for war. Blackout was compulsory and the Anderson shelter at the bottom of the garden was fully equipped and ready for occupation. Rather than being welcomed home with relief at my safe arrival, it was made clear to me that I must quickly find another bolt hole. The final explanation was that the shelter was small and unable to accommodate anyone extra.

Once again a door was closed firmly and irrecoverably. This time there seemed to be no opening beckoning me. Where could I go? What could I do? The thought of returning to chiropody filled me with dread. The war brought an end to a dream and I was overwhelmed by a total lack of confidence.

MV Inchanga - Photograph courtesy of *Shipping Today & Yesterday*

THE GRAND ORIENTAL HOTEL AND P. & O. BUILDING. COLOMBO. CEYLON.

On arriving in Colombo Pat stopped off at the Galle Face Hotel for coffee (not this hotel)

The tea factory at Hindagala

Peggy's bungalow at Hindagala

Tea picker

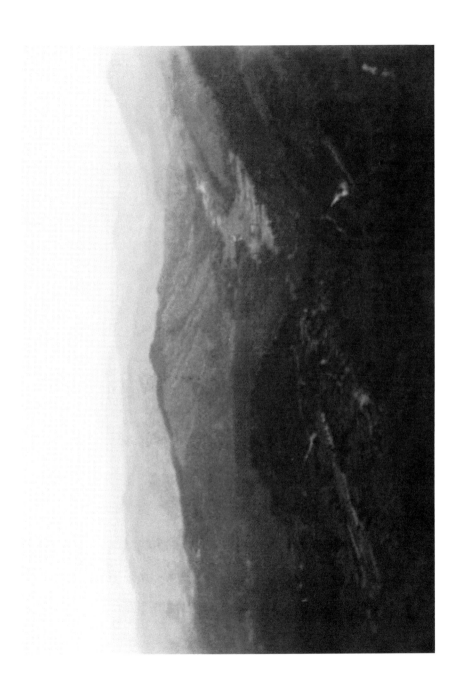

13

BEECH TREES, HASLEMERE

Amazingly, an invitation presented itself – one that I was in no position to refuse. Peter Young, who was at that time staying with his parents in Haslemere, asked me to pick up our relationship once more.

To stay with my in-laws in their beautiful house was balm to the soul. It was designed and built according to their own specifications and was surrounded by a lovely garden backed by high trees. Spacious lawns were edged with well-tended flower beds. The house had all modern conveniences, including a huge boiler for central heating. There was a feeling of lightness and airiness due to the use of light oak everywhere. This included the polished, wood-tiled floor covered with expensive carpets. Big windows brought light into the sitting room and on the sills Lilian liked to have bulbs and flowering plants in pots. Her grand piano was a central feature, and another focal point was an open fireplace that could accommodate large logs of wood.

It was soon made clear to me that this was not, for Peter, a question of marking time between jobs. The coming of the war meant that, as a conscientious objector, he had to have a plan of campaign against being called up. We decided that it would be best to find a community of like-minded people that we could join. So, having completed our preparations and made a list of communities, there came the day when we set out on our journey to a new life. We hadn't visited many communities before it became clear to Peter that he wasn't cut out for communal living and that groups of pacifists living together at close quarters were not always able to maintain a peaceful way of life.

PHOTOGRAPHS OF PAT AS A YOUNG WOMAN

PLACES AND DATES NOT KNOWN

21 April 1940

Pat with Peter Young on right

Pat on left, mother with dogs

Pat on left, father on right

At Peggy's wedding on 31 July 1937 - Father, mother and Pat

14

HOLLYSIDE, BROCKWEIR, GLOUCESTERSHIRE

It was when we were staying in Whiteway near Stroud that a change of direction began to open up. When parents heard that Peter was a teacher several of them urged him to start a small boarding school for their children. Apparently other parents had suggested this to him before, parents who wanted their children away from the war or who had been called up to the forces and needed somewhere safe for their children. It was some time later when we were staying with a small Quaker community near Tintern that Peter made up his mind. Someone mentioned that there was a cottage to rent nearby so why didn't we go and see it?

On inspection Hollyside in Brockweir proved to be two cottages joined together. It was primitive in the extreme. A lean-to shed at the side comprised the scullery-cum-kitchen, which boasted a huge copper and a sink with one cold tap. The bath was on the ground floor, which had to be filled from the copper. Last but not least was an outside loo – an Elsan. But the rent was a negligible ten shillings, which we could afford, and so we moved in. A large, sunny room upstairs became a school room and an equally large room downstairs became our bed-sitting room. This left two rooms upstairs and one downstairs for dormitories.

Our first pupil was a bright little Cockney boy called Phillip Osborne. Pip's home was in London and his father was a newspaper man. He proved to be a seasoned evacuee. His first request to me was, "Can I call you Mumfy? That's what I always call them." He settled in happily with practised ease. He could often be heard singing himself to sleep with a song that revealed his family's political persuasions. It went something like, "We fly higher, higher and higher, following the Soviet star, etc."

Pip was soon followed by David Clapp, a quiet, dark-haired boy. David and Pip soon became inseparable. Before long these two children were followed by several more. Jonathan and Valerie Tidy together with Peter Demery Gabbott formed the first contingent from Whiteway, and there was Peggy Hunt from Bristol. We were bursting at the seams!

Not having a big enough dining room table we extemporized by using a door balanced on two tea chests upon which I placed a large table cloth. The children became adept at choosing a flat surface for their mugs.

Shopping in this out-of-the-way part of the world was one of the first problems which needed a fast solution. For our speciality vegetarian foods we discovered a health food shop in Bristol run by a Mr Hockey who was prepared to send us boxes by post. For milk and eggs we were supplied by the farm down the road. There was a baker who called, and another van made weekly visits which supplied our grocery and cleaning needs. With a two-burner oil stove in the scullery and an old-fashioned small range in the kitchen, cooking the meals made demands on my ingenuity – and determination! I must have been quite successful as there were no complaints and plates returned for 'seconds' were left empty at the end of the meal.

It was not long before news of our school spread around the neighbourhood and we received requests from local parents wishing their children to join our number as day pupils. Ann and Betty Wilderspin and Angela Wigham were among the first to arrive.

The time came when we had to face the fact that it wasn't possible for me to be house mother, cook and cleaner, as well as cope with the growing amount of washing and mending. Help had to be found! That was when Fanny came. She had been a pupil at the Actors' Orphanage school in Chertsey where Peter used to work for a time. She was very glad to come to us and became a real asset. She was not afraid of hard work and related well with the children.

Two unfortunate incidents led to us making the acquaintance of the local doctor, who was Egyptian. We first had to call on his help when a child from Liverpool arrived with nits in her hair. This was something quite outside our experience. By the time we discovered the truth, all the children were infected. In horror we called the doctor. He recommended paraffin, telling us this was how lice were dealt with in his country. It was very painful when it came in contact with bare skin, but it worked and after diligent applications over some days we finally had a clean bill of health.

The second time we called him was when David Clapp, returning from the farm with a bottle of milk, fell and cut his arm very badly on the broken bottle. The doctor came and with no anaesthetic proceeded to stitch up the wound. I was holding David's other hand and we both looked away, not being able to stomach the sight. I still find it difficult to believe that this could have happened! But the wound healed perfectly in a very short space of time.

We endured a very hard winter with heavy layers of snow on the roof. When the thaw set in we found that water from the roof started to leak into one of the rooms. Peter did not improve matters by climbing up onto the roof with a spade and shovelling snow away. In doing so he sliced through some lead flashing which led to a torrent of water coming into the house! It was around this time that we decided we should look for better and more spacious accommodation.

15

There were two possibilities on the horizon. There was a monastery built by Eric Gill in the Black Mountains or a beautiful manor house in the Golden Valley. We were all packed up and ready to go to the Black Mountains when Peter had a sudden change of mind. We landed up in Bacton! It was the right decision. This was a beautiful house in lovely surroundings, just right for our children and the school.

There was a large, light room with big windows and off it was a small alcove making just enough room for my small upright piano. The roomy kitchen had a big range, a pantry with a hatch into the dining room, a larder and a scullery. The kitchen is where we held our daily staff meetings around the boiler (the warmest place) first thing in the morning while drinking cups of tea. Occasionally we were deafened by Harry Ware as he riddled and fed the boiler, encouraging it to give out extra heat. Two rooms in the main building became dormitories, and by opening up more space over the coal sheds we made room for two large bedrooms. There was also a smaller one for two bunk beds between this extra wing and a washroom in the house.

Quite extensive grounds surrounded the house and to the front was a fair-sized lake. Leading off from the lake was a small brick-built pool and a stream. Cutting a deep channel the stream came out by a long drive which took you to the outer gates and a small lodge. Here Mr Herbet lived with his wife. He came with the house and was quite invaluable. He looked after the garden and when we acquired a pony he took it upon himself to care for Dilly, a young half broken-in little mare. He also took pride in teaching the children to ride. In his youth he had worked in some stables and cared for a very famous race horse.

Billy and Lorna Frater, the friends I had made on board the Inchanga while travelling up the east coast of Africa, used to send us welcome food parcels. The children were fascinated by the grape juice that came in big tins. They called it Pip, Squeak & Liquid, which was a pretty accurate description. By explanation, it needs to be said that a children's comic, popular even as far back as my childhood, ran a story depicting a dog, a peregrine and a rabbit entitled *Pip, Squeak & Wilfred*, which was attractively illustrated.

Recording life at Freemount School would fill a whole book on its own and would be too big a task for inclusion in this small biography. We stayed in the manor for the duration of the war and then went our separate ways. Two separate incidents happened, pointing to a new direction my life would take.

Anthroposophy

The first came about because of our need to find a doctor who could advise on the children's health and who also practised homeopathy. We found a doctor living in Bristol who was prepared to give advice on general, everyday problems, although of course we had to be on good terms with the local GP. This lady doctor in Bristol, who became a good friend, out of the blue suggested that I might be interested in a workshop in Stroud that was to do with some kind dance. She strongly recommended that I take part. I went with two like-minded friends and it was there that I was first introduced to Anthroposophy.

Not only did Ellie Wilke introduce me to eurythmy but, what was much more interesting to me at the time, Dr Walter Johannes Stein was giving lectures. Furthermore, he had on display a large selection of books written by Rudolf Steiner on Waldorf education.

I bought as many books as I could carry and recognised that this was a turning point in my life. It led me to later finding my way to a Waldorf teacher training course being established in a large manor house in Forest Row, Sussex which was returning from being evacuated to Minehead during the war.

New relationship

The second event came about during the time my marriage was finally falling apart and I decided to take a break to attend a course on the comparative study of religions. My wardrobe being in a state of disrepair, I took down two of the fine blue cotton curtains from the sitting room windows, made myself a smart new dress, and departed for a well-known venue in Hertfordshire, the name of which now escapes me.

The course was intensely interesting and the experience was heightened by the unusual situation of taking part in social life and meeting people away from the enclosed life of the school. Now comes the main point of this story. As I was exploring the nether regions of the building a man came towards me who was attending another course on mechanics or some such. Somehow or other we got into conversation and became very friendly. It was intoxicating to be treated like an attractive member of the opposite sex! Later this man, Peter Hague, demonstrated sufficient interest in our relationship to visit Freemount on several occasions.

Activities on V-J Day at Freemount

It was fortunate for us that our long-awaited petrol coupons arrived on Tuesday, 14th August – as though in time for us to make our arrangements for the two-day holiday! The school had been on holiday anyway, so for a whole week we had been lying around in a half-dead condition, working off the effects of a very exhausting term. To mark these days as special and out of the ordinary it was necessary to *do* something. What could we *do*? The answer came like a gift from the gods in the form of the petrol coupons.

It was not a fine day, of course, but who expects everything these days! We bundled into the car with the dogs in the back. We took sandwiches, fruit, lettuce, orange squash, sketching materials, something to read, a sun hat as well as a mac – just in case! Everything was crammed in on the floor at the back.

Long bus queues, people racing for trains staggering under loads of suitcases, perspiring back-packers – such scenes floated through my mind as we sailed down the drive in our bright blue 'compendium' complete with paraphernalia.

Never had Hereford seemed so beautiful as we scurried down the narrow, winding lanes. Never had I seen so much of it, living that claustrophobic life in Bacton during the war years – and everyone we passed was smiling!

As we drove out into the country we found ourselves on a hill that almost beat our old engine. The last half mile was done in first gear while I grimly clung on to the gear lever, having been sternly ordered to "keep it in for God's sake!"

It was a very misty day and the view at the top was not at its best I'm sure – but we enjoyed it! Only the rain forced us away. The journey down the other side of the hill was even more exciting since it was questionable whether the brakes would hold out.

On we went, stopping later to buy some apples from a young farmer who was surrounded by four children all under five years old. As he stood with two of them climbing over him and a third coming up behind he suggested I might like to buy some children too. I could see his point!

As we went on our way again we came upon a typical country scene. There was a tractor cutting a field of corn while men, women and children stood in a circle round the fast diminishing corn, yelling and shouting. A dog was standing on tiptoes waiting to see which way to run. The tractor zoomed round in ever smaller circles – then out popped a rabbit! Swift as lightning it made a dash. The dog bounded up to head it off, and everyone yelled and brandished their sticks while chasing the poor creature.

We stood and gazed in grim fascination. It seemed the rabbits didn't stand a chance. If all else failed there stood a man with a gun. But, as we watched, first one, then another little animal shot away and disappeared into the hedge. Each time they escaped we inwardly raised a cheer. It was with feelings of disbelief that we watched even the children bashing the poor wee creatures with sticks. It was a sad ending to a happy day of celebrating a return to peace.

After the breakup of the school I returned to my parents' home. Peter Hague and I continued to see each other and we even went camping together in Cornwall. A new life had begun.

Freemount Manor

Peter Young and Pat

Pat on horse

16

MICHAEL HALL TEACHER TRAINING COURSE

1946 - 1947

1945 brought the ending of the war with the attendant vast repercussions on world events. For me, overriding the joy was the trauma of the closing of Freemount School. It had taken over my life and all my energies, leaving me exhausted and devastated. This included the shattering final break up of my marriage. The fact that this left me penniless and with no prospects could have meant a state of total despair had it not been for one ray of light. I was determined, somehow or other, to be accepted on the training course for teachers connected with Michael Hall school in order to become a Waldorf school teacher.

Because it was impossible for me to raise the money for such an undertaking, it was arranged that I would pay my way by working in the kitchen and helping Mrs Swatham in the mansion, a lady who looked after the boarders. The change could not have been more complete. My heavy workload and responsibilities gave way to being a student, living in a community committed to working with or following the high ideals of Anthroposophy, the movement founded by Rudolf Steiner.

There was an emphasis on artistic subjects such as painting, sculpture, speech and eurythmy, which all proved wonderfully healing to a depleted soul. We joined the school children in celebrating the seasons and festivals so that our first term gave us the opportunity of experiencing the harvest and Christmas festivals in an entirely new way. I will never forget the morning of our last day of the Christmas term when I was awoken from a sound sleep by a group of children touring the old army huts, where we students slept, singing Christmas carols so beautifully I could have wept. I imagined that I had been transported, miraculously, to heaven!

Looking back, I am amazed to think how lucky we were in our teachers. These included Cecil Harwood, Francis Edmunds and William Mann. Elizabeth Jacobs taught speech and black and white drawing, Mrs Darrel introduced us to painting, and Elizabeth Elwell brought a new way of working with clay.

Each day was a revelation. Free from responsibility and heartbreak, the slow process of creating a new life began. Divorce. The ending of one relationship that had lasted on and off for almost twenty years. The gradual bonding with a new partner. All this meant a great deal of soul-searching, doubt – and hope.

Peter Hague and Pat

Peter, Pat, mother and father

17

BUILDING A HOUSEBOAT AT WORCESTER

Soon after Pat finished the teacher training course she married Peter Hague and in 1947 their first daughter was born. Peter began to convert an old coal barge into a houseboat for the family to live in. It was a houseboat which he "lovingly built" for them.

But finally there came the day when Peter Hague and I were able to move into the narrowboat he was building up for our home together with Lynette, our two year old daughter. The boat was moored beside a lock just outside Worcester. Conditions were primitive, but luckily it was summer. Somehow we had managed to park my parents' caravan alongside the boat and this made life possible while the building continued.

I had a bicycle with a back seat for Lynette. Once we had crossed the lock gates and retrieved my bike from the lockkeeper's shed – the lockkeeper was a Mr Davis – we were mobile and able to reach the local shop. We even ventured into Worcester.

It is really not possible to describe the process of inner transformation that had to be gone through. From having the responsible position of housekeeper and house mother, looking after the health and welfare of thirty-five children, seeing to the ordering of food, planning the meals, laundering the linen and clothes, dealing with the parents as well as dealing with daily problems, I was now in an isolated, lonely outback, camping in a canal barge in the most primitive conditions!

Just the new experience of motherhood, which awakens a new dimension to one's emotional life, meant one could be very much at the mercy of odd moods and fluctuations of feelings. It seemed inexplicable that surrounded by nature at its best, living a life that many would envy, it was possible to be a prey to moods of deep depression that came without warning or reason.

It was as I battled with these new and strange problems that Peter's father offered him the opportunity of a job in his Pyramid works, a factory in Birmingham making aluminium saucepans. This meant moving north up the canal network. We bade farewell to Mr and Mrs Davis and started on our journey up the waterways to find a mooring near to Stourbridge and Elmfield School, where I hoped to find work.

Elmfield School is a Waldorf school.

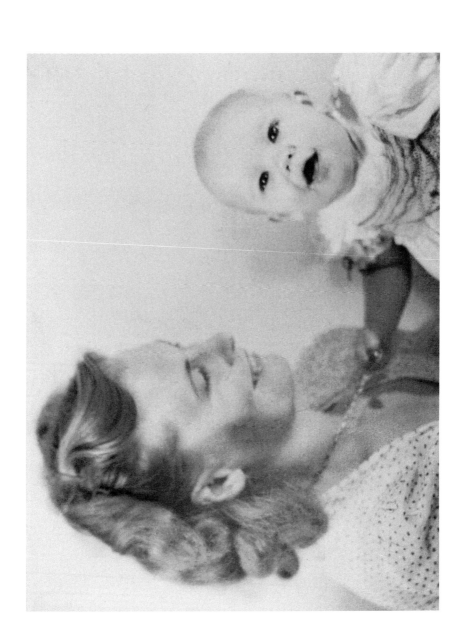

Pat, Peter Hague and Lynette

18

Kinver, Stourbridge and Elmfield School

1952 - 1972

Our first mooring in Kinver was an old coal wharf, a walled-in piece of land just below the bridge that spanned the canal. The path leading up to the road crossed on old weigh bridge beside which was a disused little office building. It was a convenient mooring place where we could safely tie up and had the advantage of a level space for the caravan. For drinking water it was necessary to cross the road to reach an outside tap behind the local pub.

So began the process of settling down to a new life in the Midlands. It was probably not such an upheaval for Peter as it was for me. He was still much involved in building up the boat, fitting in a boiler, bath, cooker and stove – we already had a proper sink and draining board. Soon Lynette was to have her own little bedroom and cot.

Peter was going back to familiar ground at the Pyramid works where he was known as the boss's son, Mr Peter. As for me, I was on foreign ground. My first trip to the village shops gave me the impression that people spoke a different language. It was impossible to understand what was being said!

With Peter away all day in Birmingham, Lynette and I lived a very isolated, primitive existence. But at least by Christmas we were warm and cosy with the boiler, cooker and stove giving out vital heat.

Looking back, it seems that the next few years just went flying by. Helena, our second child, arrived in 1950 and Lynette entered the nursery class at Elmfield School. It was not long before I joined her as a teacher, after finding someone to look after Helena and do the ironing.

Since that important time in my life when I attended the course in Stroud led by Dr Stein and was introduced to Anthroposophy, it had been my primary aim, through study and application, to further my understanding of all that this philosophy contained. By enrolling in the training course at Michael Hall I was hoping to prepare myself to become a Waldorf school teacher and so continue in the career placed upon me by circumstances. Now the situation had changed. There were two children, Lynette and Helena, for whom a Waldorf school curriculum was my primary concern. Peter was quite agreeable to the idea so long as he didn't have to foot the bill!

The first steps in my plan of campaign were now accomplished. It was the beginning of sixteen years of close association with Elmfield School as mother and teacher. It was a path of learning, inner struggle and development – but also fulfilment. My work involved relating to my colleagues as well as to the children.

Nearby in Clent was Sunfield, a home for children with special needs founded by Anthroposophists. There I went to learn eurythmy, experienced the wonderful work being done with these children through music, and enjoyed the plays put on by the co-workers.

At Elmfield there were the festivals. Midsummer brought the St John's fire festival. The Shepherds play and the Kings play were always performed at Christmas, this being the tradition in all Waldorf schools. It was all a heady and exciting life which upheld one through the long, exhausting hours of work.

KINVER, STOURBRIDGE AND ELMFIELD SCHOOL

Pat's parents bought a house for the family in Stourbridge c.1958.

We stayed in Stourbridge for fifteen years. For the last two years, after the girls had flown the nest, I attended Summerfield Teacher Training College in Kidderminster where I gained my National Teaching Diploma. This was after both my father and mother had died, leaving me with a certain financial independence.

END

Houseboat at mooring below the bridge at Kinver

View from the houseboat at mooring below the bridge

Pater holding Lynette, Pat holding Helena

View when walking along the towpath

Peter, Lynette holding Helena and Pat

The barrel in foreground is part of houseboat

Lynette, Helena and Pat

Houseboat at mooring below the bridge

Pat holding Helena, nieces Josephine and Annette with Lynette

Houseboat at mooring above the bridge which had a mains water supply

At mooring above the bridge

Pat outside house in Stourbridge

EPILOGUE

In September 1971 Pat became a teacher at St Martin's CE Primary School in Bradley, Bilston, Staffordshire. Music and art were her special subjects. In 1972 she moved south to Forest Row in Sussex with the third man in her life, Rudy Marcus. He had been a colleague at Elmfield School and shared her deep interest in Anthroposophy.

First she taught at Claremont Primary School in Tunbridge Wells. She then became a class teacher at Philpots Manor School in West Hoathly, a school which works out of the educational principles of Rudolf Steiner. She took a class from Class 2 right up to Class 8. After retiring from Philpots at 69 Pat taught remedial English at Michael Hall School and also in her own home

For the next 24 years Pat continued to be very active and formed friendships through her many interests. She attended courses at Tobias School of Art in East Grinstead and at the Hibernia School of Art in Stroud held by Karen Jarwen and Celia Whyatt. She held art sessions at the Raphael Medical Centre in Hildenborough and at home. She joined classes in eurythmy and even performed on stage at the age of 80. She was a member of Maisy Jones' poetry group for which she composed several poems. She also took part in Anthroposophical study groups.

She made many friends by letting a room to students from Emerson College. They came from all over the world as an address book she kept testifies. Pat regularly kept in touch with old scholars both from her war-time school and from Philpots right up to the end of her life.

Last but not least was her interest in the teachings of J Krishamurti. She attended his talks held in Omen, Holland in the 1930s as well as many held in the grounds of Brockwood Park School in Hampshire. Krishnamurti must have visited St Christopher School as her sister's claim to fame is playing volleyball with him there!

Reminiscences

Over the years we spent many, many hours together in the sitting room, reading or doing our own crosswords. Every now and then I would break the silence and ask her a question – about her activities or her personal views on a specific subject. Sometimes a discussion would ensue, to which she always brought a personal, spiritual dimension.

Quite often the phone would ring. Pat knew and kept in touch with a great many people; not infrequently, the caller needed counsel or a sympathetic ear. Whenever I asked her afterwards who it was, she would always give me, in a serious and compassionate tone, a very thoughtful description which revealed the essence of the person.

Often while alone with me or over dinner there would be a meditative moment, a 'thought for the day'. Pat would say something like: "Now, earlier today, when I was working in the garden, I saw . . . and then I thought . . ." One of the reasons why she never grew old was this continuous awareness, this feeling of being part of the world – and the world of nature in particular. She could observe, as well as listen. Others may have this same awareness, but Pat was a very sociable woman who wanted to share her experiences.

Unlike most of us, she never lost the child's sense of wonder. I think this was the core to her being. Every day was a fresh beginning, every event new and unique.

Knowing Pat made me understand Helena better. It also made me understand myself better. Pat has been one of the people in my life who have enlightened me. She accomplished this not by words, nor by any particular 'ism' or philosophy, but by simply being her inspiring self.

Harke Groenevelt
November 2011

Parents

Father

Capt. Archibald Campbell Goolden CBE (1879-1963) was a naval man who gave up the sea to work in the Research Department at the Royal Arsenal, Woolwich. He was a mathematician and scientist who started out in the Gunnery Department and later became superintendent.

Of the whole family my father was the shortest. His life in the navy must have been a kind of hell on earth – not only was he the victim of bullying but he also suffered from crippling seasickness. The family, however, had a kind of reverential respect for the small brother with the brains and commanding presence.

One of my first memories of him was when he was superintendent of the Research Department, a position he held for an unprecedented number of years. Peggy and I were treated like princesses when we visited occasionally on a Saturday morning. We would be taken on a tour of inspection to the different departments, quite often treated to some displays of 'special effects,' and finally seen off by the caretaker with a bunch of flowers from his garden for my mother.

A spare bedroom became his workshop, which was the most exciting glory hole you could imagine. No mop or duster, cleaner or tidier was allowed in on pain of death. This is where the magic lantern was kept and where a wireless was created that fed through to every other room in the house.

My father spent his life measuring up to people and to tasks. To make up for his lack of inches (which he put down to being immersed in a scalding bath as a toddler) he had to succeed – he had to win! No matter what the game – he won! No matter what the job he undertook – he came out on top! This underlay the modest, shy man who was kindly and warm-hearted and wouldn't hurt a fly. Many people, not just family, came to him for help and advice.

He had a great sense of duty. He was also a stickler for detail – his eye missed nothing! One of his responsibilities was to tour munitions factories during the war. When he found careless, shoddy work his fury was unmistakeable. Management shook in its shoes whenever he appeared!

Mother

Janet Keith Goolden (née Stannus) (1879-1962) was the only child of an artist from Belfast, Anthony Carey Stannus. Her mother died shortly after giving birth and the baby was left in charge of a real old 'Mother Gamp' who put gin in her feed to keep her quiet. Luckily an aunt, together with her mother, came to visit from Australia. Finding an impossible situation, Nora Peacock took charge. She fired the nurse and proceeded to care for the infant and provide for its well-being herself.

I'm not sure how long it was before Antonio, the father, returned home to shoulder his responsibilities, nor am I sure how long Nora stayed with the child. But there came a time when Nora's mother told her that it was time to return to Australia.

It came to pass that Antonio found a farmer and his wife willing to look after his daughter. Here she lived a primitive, peasant existence together with the children of the family. That was until her maternal uncle found her and threatened to remove her to safety if her father did not provide for her properly.

Again her life was transformed. She was taken to live with Antonio's maiden sister in Carrick Fergus. She learnt to wear shoes and starched frocks. Her hair was tied back so hard her eyes watered. There was church twice on Sundays and plenty of rules and regulations.

When she became a teenager Antonio finally decided he must have a hand in her upbringing. He took her to live with him in Brighton and sent her to school. This was a difficult step for Janet, who had had no previous schooling and came with a broad Irish accent.

Father

Mother

PEOPLE IN MY EARLY LIFE

Father's relatives

My father had five brothers and three sisters.

Walter *married* Lucy Plater
   No children

Lucy's sister, Evie, *married* Gerald
   Son: Tim

Kitty *married* Harry Nicholson *(lived in India)*
   Children: Jan, Joan

Archie *married* Netta Stannus
   Children: Margaret (Peggy), Katharine (Pat)

Dorothy *married* Bob Coomb *(lived in Ceylon)*
   Children: Rosemary, John, Dick

Dick *married* Olive *(lived in South Africa)*
   Children: Jack, Peter

Enid *single*

Cyril *married* Eustine (Tinny) *(lived in Ceylon)*
   Children: Marjory, Douglas

Guy *married* Madeleine
   Daughter: Peggy

Hugo *married* Sheila
   Daughter: Shirley

Mother's relatives

Aunt Nora Peacock from Australia came to visit occasionally.

Our household at different times

Mr & Mrs Mac *(gardener & cook)*
Mr Thrush *(gardener)*
Violet Philips *(maid of all work)*
Dorothy Borket *(cook)*
Mrs Bridgeman (Bridgie) *(cook)*
Olé *(au pair)*
Ginger Greaves *(governess)*
Milly *(maid of all work)*

Our animals

Coo-ee *(dog)*
George *(dog)*
Sally (dog)
Peggy Pony *(pony)*
Hetty and Jane *(hens)*

Neighbours

Col. Dick Baines & Mrs Baines *(neighbours at Beechbrook)*
Janet and Dick *(killed on the NW Frontier)*
Mrs Straus
Mr & Mrs Scott
Tim Buster
Miss Lavender
Madelaine and Ursula Wheen *(hockey)*
Dr White and daughters Violet & Helen *(nursing home)*
Dr Pink *(nursing home)*
Mr & Mrs Levy, Tony & Patrick *(farm in Kent)*

Coed Bel School

Mary Munroe
Audrey Rice
Helen Fox

Dancing classes

Mrs Grant *(dance teacher at the Bell Hotel)*

Piano lessons

Miss Davis

Riding lessons

Mr English

Research Department, Woolwich

Sir Robert Robertson KBE FRS (1869-1949)
(Knighted for his research during the Great War)
Sir Alwyn Crow CBE FInstP (1894-1965)
(In 1917 he was appointed to the staff of the Royal Arsenal, Woolwich. He was Director of Ballistics Research at Woolwich 1919-39. He was Knighted in 1944) (Wikipedia)
Dr Godfrey Rotter CB CBE (1879-1969)
Col. Herbert Parcell (the Funny Man – his wife was Tibs)
Mrs Clement Long
N Pullen
S Rees
H Pristen

St Christopher School – Students

Hotstuff

Mary Soutar
Dorothy Swan
Joan Hyde
Me
Joan Duckworth
Brenda Sayers

Little Hotstuff

Nada Howard Flanders
Billie Bennett

My Group

Joan Hyde
Dorothy Swan
Shanta Bignold
Michael Muir
Audrey Gibson
Jean Lavender
John Fennel
Mary Souter
Chris Tudor Pole
David Barker

Lower Group

Billie Bennett
Nada Howard Flanders
Joan Nicholson
David Knaggs
Joan Duckworth
Maurice Beckett

Middle Group

David Soutar
Dennis Coombes
Magnus Pearce
Alan Young
Phyllis Dax
Victoria Driver
Enid Ferrybough
Peggy Goolden
Dennis Brook

Upper Group

Lillie Lewellyn
Gilbert Leslie
Geoffrey Parker
Jack Austin
Peter Young
Rosemary Hewitt
Ruth Kellaway
Celine
Audrey
Marie Frans

St Christopher School – Staff

Lyn Harris *(headmaster)*
Mrs Brook *(art)*
Elsie Brooks *(gym, games)*
Mrs Backet *(cooking)*
Mr Cuckoo *(maths)*
Miss Elvis *(house mother)*
Mr Ferrybough *(science)*
Miss Hargreaves *(domestic studies)*
Nora Knaggs *(Dalcroze eurhythmics)*
Mr Little *(French)*

Max Morton *(history)*
James Potter *(geography)*
Winifred Swan *(natural movement)*
Dorothy Sergeant
Simone Sermon *(English, French)*
Reg Snell *(German)*
Miss Taylor *(piano)*
Mr White *(maths)*

RADA (Royal Academy of Dramatic Art)

Teachers

Dorothy Green (1892-1963)
Sara Allgood (1879-1950)
Mme Gashet
Irene Vanbrurgh (1872-1949)
Violet Vanbrugh (1867-1942)

Students at same time as Pat

Trevor Howard (1913-1988)
Howard Marion-Crawford (1914-1969)
Margaret Lockwood (1916-1990)

Hollyside – A school for evacuee children

Boarders

Philip Osbourne *(our first pupil)*
David Clapp
Jonathan Tidy *(from Whiteway Colony)*
Valerie Tidy *(from Whiteway Colony)*
Peter Demery Gabbott *(from Whiteway Colony)*
Ian Holmes
Peggy Hunt

Day Pupils

Betty Withespoon
Ann Withespoon
Angela Wigham
Rollo Aisbet and sister

Helpers

Fanny
  (She came from the Actors' Orphanage where Peter once worked)
Mary Wild

Freemount – A school for evacuee children

Andrew Zobel *(helper)*

Angela Whyham

Ann Leatherbarrow

Donald

Anthony Bristow

Armene Ware

Charles Ware

Chef

Cynthia Proud

David Clapp

David Walters

Donne Parsons

Gerald Williams

Gillian Lunnon

Giovanni Rossi

Gloria Calvert

Harry Ware

Humphrey Booth

Irene Glover

Jane Gaudin

Mark Gaudin

Jane Maynard

Jill churchman

Jill Glover

Jill Richards

John Cave

John Gilbert

John Lambert

Jonathan Tidy

June Blue

Kathleen Nissim

Keith Payne

Lao Holland

Madeleine Holland *(helper)*

Mary Smith

Mary Wild *(helper)*

Morgan Griffith Thomas

Mr Herbert *(caretaker)*

Mrs Peachy *(helper)*

Nanette Clench

Patsy Jackson

Patsy Jackson

Paul Hadley

Peggy Hunt

Peter Demery Gabbott

Peter Hamilton Clark

Philip Osborne

Pierce Weber

Rosemary McClaughlin

Seamus Stuart

Sonia Read

Susan Watts

Tom Glover

Tony Lunnon

Tyl Kennedy

Valorie Tidy

Valya Boss

Wendy Gabbott

Willy Holland

Anthroposophical course

Dr Walter Johannes Stein *(lectures)*
Ellie Wilke *(eurythmy)*

Teacher training course at Michael Hall

Cecil Harwood *(lectures)*
Francis Edmunds *(lectures)*
William Mann *(lectures)*
Elizabeth Jacobs *(speech, black & white drawing)*
Mrs Darrel *(painting)*
Elizabeth Elwell *(clay)*
Mrs Swatham *(house mother)*

On houseboat at Worcester

Mr & Mrs Davis *(lockkeeper and his wife)*

BOOKS FROM CHILDHOOD

A Girl of the Limberlost – Gene Stratton-Porter
A Princess of Mars – Edgar Rice Burroughs
A Tale of Two Cities – Charles Dickens
A Yankee at the Court of King Arthur – Mark Twain
Allan Quartermain – Henry Rider Haggard
Alice in Wonderland – Lewis Carroll
Alice Through the Looking Glass – Lewis Carroll
At the Back of the North Wind – George Macdonald
Black Beauty – Anna Sewell
Daddy Long-Legs – Jean Webster
David Copperfield – Charles Dickens
Finn and the Fianna – (Irish mythology)
Freckles – Gene Stratton-Porter
Grimms' Fairy Tales – (folklore)
Gulliver's Travels – Jonathan Swift
Hajji Baba of Isphan – James Morier
Jane Eyre – Charlotte Brontë
King Arthur and His Knights of the Round Table – (Legend)
King Solomon's Mines – Henry Rider Haggard
Little Women – Louisa May Alcott
Lorna Doone – R D Blackmore
Nada the Lilly – Henry Rider Haggard
Old St Paul's – William Harrison Ainsworth
Peter Rabbit – Beatrix Potter
Pilgrim's Progress – John Bunyan
Quentin Durwood – Sir Walter Scott
Riders of the Purple Sage – Zane Grey
Robin Hood – (English folklore)
She – Henry Rider Haggard
Sylvie and Bruno – Lewis Carroll
Tarzan the Ape-Man – Edgar Rice Burroughs

The Adventures of Huckleberry Finn – Mark Twain
The Ancient Mariner – Samuel Taylor Coleridge
The Arabian Nights – (legend)
The Broad Highway – Jeffery Farnol
The Call of the Wild – Jack London
The Christmas Carol – Charles Dickens
The Heroes – Charles Kingsley
The Jungle Book – Rudyard Kipling
The Prince and the Pauper – Mark Twain
The Red Cockade – Stanley Weyman
The Song of Hiawatha – Longfellow
The Water Babies – Charles Kingsley
Thirty Nine Steps – John Buchan
Uncle Tom's Cabin – Harriet Beecher Stone
Westwood Ho! – Charles Kingsley
Wuthering Heights – Emily Brontë

PLACES FROM CHILDHOOD

Chislehurst Caves
Petts Wood *(William Willett Daylight Saving Time 1916)*
St Mary's Cray
St Paul's Cray
Foot's Cray

Picnic areas

Sidcup
Sevenoaks
Westerham
Wrotham
Farnborough